INVASION

*Saddam Hussain's reign of
terror in Kuwait*

A didication to
MR. Gordon E. Whyte
with my best wishes

Ali
18·1·94

D1488730

HOLY QURAN

It is He who got out the unbelievers among the People of the Book from their homes at the first gathering (of the forced). Little did ye think that they would get out: and they thought that their fortresses would defend them from God! But the (wrath of) God came to them from quarters from which they little expected (it) and cast terror into their hearts, so that they destroyed their dwellings by their own hands and the hands of the believers. Take warning, then, oh ye with eyes (to see)!

Al-Hashr Surah (2)

Remember! Moses said to his people: "Call to mind the favour of God to you when He delivered you from the people of Pharaoh: They set you hard tasks and punishments, slaughtered your sons, and let your womenfolk live: therein was a tremendous trial from your Lord."

And remember! Your Lord caused to be declared (publicly): "If ye show ingratitude, truly my punishment is terrible indeed."

Ibrahim Surah (6-7)

INVASION

Saddam Hussain's reign of terror in Kuwait

BY ALI MOHAMED AL-DAMKHI, Ph.D.

Kuwait Research and Advertising Co. Ltd.
65 Uxbridge Road, Ealing, London. W5 5SA, UK

© Kuwait Research and Advertising Co. Ltd.
65 Uxbridge Road, London W5 5SA, UK.

Second published 1992

ISBN   0 9518857 0 7

The majority of photographs appearing in
this book were taken by the author

Printed by Dubai Printing Press, U.A.E.

CONTENTS

DEDICATION

To the symbol of legitimacy and resistance, the Amir of Kuwait HH Shaikh Jaber Al-Ahmed Al-Sabah who carried Kuwait's torment in his heart despite the pain.

To the Crown Prince and Prime Minister HH Shaikh Saad Al-Abdullah Al-Salem Al-Sabah who throughout the months of occupation stood like a strong mountain and led us down the path to liberation.

To the martyrs of Kuwait who gave their blood in order that their country regain its freedom.

To the children of Kuwait who silently endured all kinds of torture.

To the people of Kuwait who experienced fear, hunger and terror for their country's sake.

To the people of Kuwait who carried Kuwait's message to the rest of the world.

To their Highnesses the leaders of the Gulf Co-operation Council countries who wrote a chapter in their history of sacrifice and loyalty to Kuwait throughout the occupation and liberation.

To our brothers in the Gulf, Egypt and Syria who opened their hearts and homes to Kuwaitis.

To the leaders and peoples of Islamic and friendly countries who stood up for the truth and assisted Kuwait against injustice.

To President Bush and former British Prime Minister Margaret Thatcher.

To those in the coalition countries who laid down their lives for the sake of Kuwait.

To all of these I dedicate this book

INVASION
Saddam Hussain's reign of terror in Kuwait

Ali Mohamed Al-Damkhi Ph.D.

HH The Amir Shaikh Jaber Al-Ahmad Al-Sabah arriving in Free Kuwait on 14 March 1991.

Working hand in hand with the people to rebuild Kuwait.

HH The Crown Prince Shaikh Saad Al-Abdullah Al-Salem Al-Sabah arriving home on 4 March 1991 with a salute for the people and a pledge of a new Kuwait

ABOUT THE AUTHOR

Ali Mohamed Al-Damkhi was born in Kuwait in 1958. He graduated with a B.Sc. in June 1981 from the Faculty of Engineering & Petroleum at Kuwait University. In 1986 Dr Al-Damkhi received a Ph.D. in chemical engineering at Aston University, Birmingham, in the UK. For five years (1982-87) the author was Head of the Department of Environmental Studies for Projects at the Ministry of Health's Environment Protection Council. Since 1987 he has been attached to the Department of Environmental Health in the Public Authority for Applied Education and Training as assistant professor. In January 1990 he was appointed director of the authority's scholarship and cultural affairs department. Dr Al-Damkhi is a consultant to the Regional Organisation for the Protection of the Marine Environment having studied pollution in the UAE and Kuwait. He presented a TV programme (Made in Kuwait) which was shown on local television. He has been a frequent speaker at conferences and seminars on the environment and industry. He was appointed to the ministerial committee formed on the orders of the Cabinet to deal with oil fires after liberation.

ALI MOHAMED AL-DAMKHI, Ph.D

PREFACE

The invasion of Kuwait on 2 August 1990 was the biggest armed robbery in history. Crime on a grand scale is perhaps far too inadequate an expression to describe an attempt to eliminate an entire nation. Many parts of this account of the occupation were written during the seven month nightmare which lasted until liberation on 26 February 1991. I was determined that there should be a record of Saddam Hussain's misdeeds in Kuwait in words, photographs and documents. This is my eyewitness report on the 208-day occupation.

I was one of the reservists who answered the call to arms on 2 August 1990 and fought through one of the most hard fought engagements -- the siege of Jiwan Camp. Thanks to God's grace I survived but hundreds of others lost their lives in defence of Kuwait.

This description of life in Kuwait during the occupation is necessarily subjective but it covers not only atrocities and human rights abuses but reveals the full and cynical masterplan to erase Kuwait's identity as a nation and steal its heritage. The Iraqi attempt at a "final solution" to destroy Kuwait and its people failed, but only thanks to the solidarity shown by its citizens and the support which was forthcoming from Arab, Islamic and friendly powers.

I wish to extend my sincere and heartfelt thanks to H.H. the Crown Prince and Prime Minister Shaikh Saad Al-Abdullah Al-Salem Al-Sabah who supported the idea of the Arabic version of this book project; H.E. Shaikh Salem Sabah Al-Salem, Deputy Prime Minister and Foreign Minister for his continuous encouragement; H.E. Shaikh Ali Sabah Al-Salem, Minister of Defence, who supported the idea of this book project materially and morally. H.E. the Minister of Information Dr Badr Jassim Al-Yakoub facilitated its printing.

H.E. Shaikh Sabah Al-Nasser Al-Saud Al-Sabah gave me much valuable information about the crisis. H.E. Kuwait's Deputy Chief-of-Staff General Jaber Al-Khalid Al-Sabah supplied a collection of photographs of the martyrs.

I also wish to thank the following individuals: Shaikh Faisal Al-Malik Al-Humood Al-Sabah; Colonel Sultan Al-Ramyan; Lieutenant-Colonel Abdul-Karim Al-Gharabally; Lieutenant-Colonel Derbas Al-Haddad; Lieutenant-Colonel Khalid Saoud Al-Fadel; Lieutenant-Colonel Fahd Al-Khamiri; Dr Waleed Bishara; Engineer Waleed Abdullah Al-Awadi; Waleed Al-Loughany; Adnan Al-Ameeri; As'ad Ahmed Abdullah; Mish'al Al-Saq'ubi; Ahmed Shams El-dein; Dr Yousif Ahmed Al-Nisf; Miss Moodhi Al-Miftah; Marwan Mohamed Al-Saleh; and Khalid Mahmoud Al-Fajji.

I am also grateful to Dr Mohammed Al-Rumaihi, Anwar Al-Yaseen, John Whelan and Roger Emmerson of Kuwait Research & Advertising Ltd for their assistance with the English version.

Ali Mohamed Al-Damkhi, Ph.D.
December 1991

LIST OF COLOUR PLATES

SADDAM'S CONSPIRACY AGAINST KUWAIT

"IRAQI FORCES BROKE THROUGH THE NORTHERN BORDERS OF KUWAIT AT DAWN TODAY. WE SHALL BROADCAST MORE DETAILS AS SOON AS WE RECEIVE THEM"

This was the first news flash about the invasion broadcast by Kuwait Radio in its main 6.00 a.m. bulletin by newscaster Mahmood Saqr on Thursday 2 August 1990. His words came like a thunderbolt to me - for a moment I couldn't believe my ears.

What had happened? Could it be true? I waited for the next news report for confirmation. The unthinkable had occurred... something Kuwait's leaders and citizens had always considered beyond the realms of possibility.

The hatred felt by Iraq's dictator towards Kuwait finally revealed itself in its true colours during those dark morning hours of 2 August 1990, while the peaceloving Kuwaiti people were asleep in their beds, but was this something sudden - a momentary impulse? The answer is an emphatic - No!

The circumstantial evidence of Iraq's aggressive intentions towards Kuwait had been sufficient to generate suspicion and fear of Baghdad, not only in the minds of Kuwait's rulers but also among its people.

Yet there were contrary signals.

Kuwait's political leaders had been anxious to foster good neighbourliness and had heeded the counsel of King Fahd of Saudi Arabia and Egypt's President Mubarak. These two statesmen had assured H.H. The Amir of Kuwait that there would be no Iraqi military action against Kuwait.

Indeed Iraq had awarded the Amir its highest decoration of honour. An attack seemed inconceivable, despite the evidence to the contrary. The facade of Iraq's so called good intentions was indeed a cruel sham. Instead the events that followed 2 August 1990 - the tragedy of Kuwait - were to reveal a carefully drawn and well executed plan to destroy an entire nation state.

▶ *Anniversary speech of 17 July 1990*

I was with my military unit serving as a lieutenant in the Kuwaiti army reserve on the morning of Tuesday 17 July 1990. Although I was on my annual refresher course, I learned that half the forces had been put on full alert by the Chief of Staff, among them my own.

Most officers failed to grasp the reason for this. A discussion ensued and it didn't take long for everyone to get to the message. The alarm resulted from President Saddam Hussain of Iraq's speech to celebrate the anniversary of the Ba'athist Revolution (17-30 July).

His words flagged up the evil motives which most members of Saddam's government were contemplating against Kuwait. He blamed the "economic crisis" facing Iraq on Kuwait and the United Arab Emirates which he accused of exceeding OPEC oil production quotas and seeking to drive down crude oil prices.

Saddam Hussain's regime continued its campaign against Kuwait when the Foreign Minister Tariq Hanna Aziz filed a memorandum with the Arab League alleging that Kuwait had exploited the circumstances of the Iran-Iraq war (1980-88), had stolen $2.5 billion in Iraqi crude from the geologically shared Rumaila field and had constructed a military post on Iraqi territory.

At the same time the Iraqi government launched a propaganda drive against Kuwait aimed at transferring the blame for Iraq's economic collapse from Saddam Hussain's eight year war with Iran to the innocent Kuwaitis. Saddam told television audiences that "oil shaikhs" were to blame for poverty in Iraq and that the Gulf states, Kuwait in particular, were bent on humiliating Baghdad.

Sadly, many Iraqis believed their dictator, with the result that a military adventure was launched that would kill more than 7,000 Kuwaitis, send into exile hundreds of thousands of people during the occupation and result in 25,000 people being listed as missing. Those were the figures released by the Kuwaiti ambassador to Washington Shaikh Saud Nasser Al-Sabah in an interview with American network television on 27 October 1990.

▶ *Military build-up*

From the second week in July 1990, international and Arab news agencies broadcast news of huge Iraqi military concentrations on the northern Kuwaiti border. Estimates of their numbers ranged from 120,000-170,000.

Some Kuwaitis returning home from Iraq gave me eyewitness reports of what they had seen in southern Iraq. They concluded that the build-up was for real and not just "sabre rattling" as predicted in press reporting. The army was equipped with artillery, rocket launchers and tanks. Iraqi soldiers would wave at passing Kuwaiti motorists and shout:"Look out, we're on our way." A friend with relatives in Basra reported that the build-up had started there in the second week in June - six weeks before the attack.

These stories tend to confirm a claim by one Kuwaiti official that Saddam Hussain had planned his final attack on Kuwait some time previously, possibly after receiving a note from the Kuwait Government in May 1990 requesting repayment of loans.

I have no doubt that the financial memorandum may have been the straw that broke the camel's back. It enraged Saddam and made him take leave of his senses but history will also bear witness to the boldness of the Kuwaiti government. It claimed what was due to Kuwait in plain and blunt terms being mindful of the delaying tactics and reputation for blackmail acquired over many years by the Ba'athist government in Baghdad.

▶ *Border problems*

The delineation of the Kuwait-Iraq boundary is an outstanding problem which has preoccupied every Iraqi regime from the 1960s onwards, with no solution as yet. The only explanation of this long delay lies with the Ba'athist government's arrogance, its desire to blackmail Kuwait and plan to use Kuwait as a milch cow.

The Iraqi journalist Hassan Al-Alawi summed up official thinking by declaring that "Kuwait must be seen as a cash till for our economy."

Indeed Kuwait had supported Iraq in its long war with Iran, giving money and ammunition for eight years and paying out again for the reconstruction of the township of Fao and other areas devastated by war. But to what end? Let's remember the Arabic proverb:" Beware of those to whom you give charity."

It is to be regretted that the tyrant of Baghdad failed to appreciate Kuwait's support during his self-made crisis (the Iraq-Iran war) but acted instead in a way which re-vealed the hate he harboured against Kuwait.

Even the visits by H.H. The Amir and H.H. the Crown Prince of Kuwait after the end of the Iraq-Iran war, failed to achieve a breakthrough, especially over the border dispute. About that time Kuwaiti editors when going to interview Saddam Hussain were banned by the Iraqi authorities from asking questions about the mutual border. Hamad Jassim Al-Sa'eed, editor-in-chief of the daily Al-Raie Al Aaam broke this embargo and posed the key issue.

Saddam Hussain responded:" The boundary problem is a difficult one. Our land is overlapping your land. Leave this matter alone for a while. Let time solve it. We are after all brothers."

Later he added:" Why do we need to solve the border issue. Kuwait's borders extend as far as Baghdad and our's reach as far as Kuwait (City)."

What Saddam Hussain said was indeed rhetorically true, in the language of pan-Arabism but his actual words were laced with falsehood. The rejection and postponement of border talks, and the Iraqi refusal to delineate borders were clear signals that the government in Baghdad intended to flout this matter and exploit it, as proved later by the invasion and occupation of Kuwait.

▶ *Response to Iraqi claims*

For a long time Kuwait turned the other cheek towards Iraq in the interests of Arab unity but finally Iraqi Foreign Minister Tariq Aziz overstepped the mark by claiming that: "Kuwait failed to provide Iraq with anything during its (1980-88) crisis but attempted instead to choke and humiliate us."

Kuwait then abandoned its policy of silence. In a communique of 17 July 1990 Kuwait's former Foreign Minister Shaikh Sabah Al-Ahmed set out the material and moral support provided by Kuwait to Iraq at all levels. Ordinary Kuwaitis were astounded by the document's frankness.

From his accession in 1978 to the present time H.H. The Amir of Kuwait Shaikh Jaber Al-Ahmed has endured many crises and difficulties during which he had the full backing of his people and government. Firmness has been a characteristic of the Amir's style of crisis management. The following are a few examples of outrages inflicted on Kuwait:

- *Five bomb explosions in December 1983*
- *Hijacking of the Kuwait Airways Corporation Airbus "Kazima" in December 1984*
- *Attack on the Amir's cavalcade in May 1985*
- *Bomb attacks on public cafes in the summer of 1987 in which many innocent Kuwaitis and expatriates were killed*
- *The 16-day hijacking of the KAC Boeing 747 "Al-Jaberiyya" in April 1988 which ended with the terrorists surrendering in Algiers.*

There were in addition certain mysterious incidents, such as the attack on the Rawdatain oilfield and the shelling of an artificial island, as well as the destruction of Kuwaiti oil tankers in the Iran-Iraq war.

It is now clear that the Iraqi government covertly planned most of these incidents or encouraged the fifth columnists who executed them inside or outside Kuwait. At the time Kuwait was governed by a desire to spare bloodshed and give Iraq the benefit of the doubt. For that reason Kuwait always acted prudently but by mid- July 1990 the situation had become intolerable.

▶ *Iraqi embassy in Kuwait*

The events of 2 August 1990 exposed our suspicions about the role of Iraq's embassy in Kuwait in preparing for the attack. Many secret agents had been planted by Iraqi Intelligence in strategic installations. A friend claims that the Iraqi Embassy in Kuwait had more than 2,000 people on the payroll but only 20 of them were accredited diplomats. The others worked for the secret service. Kuwaitis were astounded to discover after the invasion how many Iraqi agents had been working alongside them in government departments, institutions and companies.

The Kuwaiti Ministry of Interior became alarmed when the Iraqis put in a block application for No Objection Certificates to cover 400 people a short time before the invasion. The Iraqi Embassy abused the privileged diplomatic access it had to the Ministry of Interior to import these op-

The Iraqi Embassy in Kuwait - played an underhand role in the invasion

eratives to take up a pre-assigned role in the invasion plan.

▶ *The Jeddah Conference-pretext for aggression*

When the Kuwait-Iraq crisis escalated in the last week of July, King Fahd of Saudi Arabia, the Custodian of the Two Holy Mosques, convened a meeting between the two parties to discuss outstanding bilateral issues. Kuwait responded warmly to the Saudi initiative and the meeting took place in Jeddah under the auspices of H.H. Crown Prince Abdullah Ibn Abdul-Aziz, First Deputy Prime Minister and head of the National Guard. Kuwait's delegation was led by H.H. the Crown Prince and Prime Minister Shaikh Saad Al-Abdullah Al-Salem Al-Sabah and more than 60 officials, among them former Oil Minister Dr Rasheed Salem Al-Ameeri. By contrast the Iraqi delegation was headed by Vice-Chairman of the Revolution Command Council Izzat Ibrahim Al-Doori and not more than five aides.

The Kuwaiti delegation attended with an open mind and a true desire to resolve all outstanding issues between the two countries through dialogue and negotiation. Were the Iraqis attending the meeting in the same spirit? In fact, Izzat Ibrahim Al-Doori and his team were mere parrots there to repeat their master's words. They had no mandate to negotiate or agree a compromise. I was at the "diwaniya" of former Minister of State for Housing Engineer Yahya Al-Sumait on the evening

HH The Crown Prince Shaikh Saad shaking hands with Izzat Al-Doori - six hours later the invasion was launched

of 1 August 1990, the day the Kuwaiti delegation returned from Jeddah, when I heard that all H.H. Shaikh Saad's efforts had been in vain. Jeddah was no Munich - the occasion when the allies appeased Hitler before World War II. The Iraqis had only attended as a cover for their real intentions - to launch an attack on Kuwait a few hours after the end of the meeting.

Plate 1. The Iraqi Embassy in Kuwait

Plate 2. Marble plaque at the entrance to the Iraqi embassy opened in 1980

Plate 3. Iraqi helicopters fill the Kuwaiti sky on the morning of 2 August 1990

SIG 1 (1)

8

Plate 4. An Iraqi warplane downed in Hawalli

Plate 5. The southern entrance to Jiwan Camp

Plate 6. The main entrance to Jiwan Camp where the battle started

Plate 7. The Ministry of Electricity & Water - the Iraqis used the roof as an observation post to attack Jiwan Camp

Plate 8. Iraqi troops with their equipment in the Al-Massilah area on the first day of the occupation

Plate 9. A National Guard Armoured Personnel Carrier which had been protecting the Dasman Palace

Plate 10. The Crown Prince's palace in Sha'ab - attacked twice on 2 August 1990 by Iraqi aircraft

Plate 11. The martyr Shaikh Fahd Al-Ahmed's car near the Dasman Palace's western gate

Plate 12. Damage at the Ministry of Information complex

Plate 13. Equipment used for clandestine radio broadcasts

Plate 14. Shaikh Mohamed Yousif Al-Sabah's palace - site of a secret radio broadcasting station

Plate 15. A file of Iraqi tanks which took part in the invasion

DEFENDING KUWAIT TO THE LAST

In the Kuwaiti "diwaniyas" for the two weeks before the invasion endless questions were posed about Iraq. Was it possible for Saddam Hussain to accuse Kuwait so openly of stealing oil from the Rumaila field? Was it acceptable to deploy huge troop concentrations near the border and claim they were on manoeuvres? What was the significance of the hate campaign against Kuwait in the Iraqi media?

Kuwaitis debated these issues but still clung to the belief that Saddam Hussain would forbid a single shot to be fired against Kuwait. After all Kuwaitis knew how much money had been emptied into the Iraqi finance ministry. Even Saddam's own pocket bulged with billions of dollars of Kuwaiti money. Kuwaitis could scarcely entertain the notion that Saddam would unleash his hordes on them -- the very people with whom the Saudis had built up Iraq's arsenal over the past eight years. They said it was out of character for an Arab to bite the hand that feeds him, especially that of the state which had helped rebuild Fao and Basra after

The car belonging to the martyr Shaikh Fahd Al-Ahmed with a bullet penetrating the windscreen

12

Kuwaiti women abroad - their resilience and courage were proved after the invasion

they were destroyed by war. It was a grave miscalculation.

▶ *Foreign warplanes in the sky*

At 5.30 a.m. on 2 August 1990 I awoke to the scream of interceptors shattering the dawn silence. I climbed to my roof to observe and watched two fighter bombers flying high speed at low level. The walls of the house shivered. Overhead the aircrafts' profile was foreign to me. Their livery was grey with a red, black and white flag. They were approaching from the south-west of Kuwait traversing towards the north-east opposite Salmiyah. It was the enemy. I came down quickly and tuned to Kuwait Radio news. The "tyrant of Baghdad" had invaded Kuwait.

I immediately changed into military uniform and jumped into my car, tuned again to Kuwait Radio and sped off to join my unit at Jiwan Camp. I was supposed to get my demob papers that morning after completing my annual 28 days training course so I could return to civilian life on Saturday 4 August 1990.

Events were unfolding that would turn the clock back for many Kuwaitis. On the 5th Ring Road, from its junction with the Fahaheel Motorway to the Rabia traffic lights near the second hand car mart, traffic was moving normally, except for three Amiri Guard vehicles, in their distinguishing red livery, besides which Kuwaiti soldiers were stationed. They were blocking the northern entrance to the Bayan Palace which overlooks the 5th Ring Road. It was 0645 in the morning. Kuwait Radio's FM transmission ceased abruptly but continued on 540 khz medium wave.

▶ Defence of Jiwan Camp

Arriving at Jiwan Camp's southern entrance, I at once observed the state of alert. It confirmed not only the Iraqi penetration of the northern frontier, as reported on radio, but the presence of the invading forces in Kuwait City. A lieutenant-colonel was checking the I.D. of people entering the camp. Two soldiers with automatic weapons and fingers on the trigger were guarding the side platforms above the entrance. After passing muster I entered the camp and reported for duty. It was 0700 and a surprise awaited me. I was the first reserve officer recruit to report.

Captain Hussein Al-Adwani ordered me, with obvious signs of confusion on his face, to change immediately from dress to field uniform and collect whatever arms and ammunition were available from the armoury. When I requested permission to return home quickly to collect my kit the captain replied:" If you can get out..."

He added that Iraqi Republican Guard units were blocking Jiwan Camp from the north and west and were now close to Army Staff Headquarters' northern gate.

I cannot describe my emotions at that moment. I was bewildered. Fear and hope alternated -- concern about the unknown and a belief that what I was hearing would turn out false. Many questions flashed through my mind. Was it possible that the Iraqi forces could reach Kuwait City so quickly? Was it my fate to die here? Would God's grace allow me to survive?

Just then Major Ali Al-Kandari, an officer of the unit, entered the room, He was unaware of what was going on around us. I reported:"Iraqi forces are near the entrance to headquarters, Sir!" He didn't believe me and telephoned the ops rooms. The officer in charge confirmed my report.

To quell the growing confusion, Major Al-Kandari ordered volunteers, reserve officers and recruits to gather round for a briefing. He began reading Military Announcement No 1 issued by Jiwan Camp's ops room. It declared: "All officers and other ranks of army units in the camp are ordered to stand-by on red alert."

Red alert meant war. The instructions now were to issue guns and ammunition and protect the unit's buildings from the outside but not to muster in case the building came under enemy artillery attack.

▶ Fight to the last

At about 0830 I heard incoming shell fire aimed at the camp from the west near the Police College. A group of Kuwaiti officers and men from a number of different units crossed our lines in search of weapons and ordnance. The main armoury's supply was exhausted and confusion again reigned due to contradictory military orders.

The ops room had instructed that weapons were to be surrendered and no fire was to be directed at the enemy. Officers and men began handing over weapons and ordnance to a lieutenant. The headquarters ops room had decided that the Iraqi deployments blocking Jiwan hugely outnumbered us in personnel and equipment. I concurred with that difficult decision. The ratio of men in the Kuwaiti and Iraqi armies was a comparison of 1:33. Given such odds, it was a no win situation for Kuwait.

Less than an hour later one of the 15th Brigade commanders arrived. Colonel Mohamed Al-Haramy reached Jiwan Camp accompanied by a number of tanks and requested all officers and men available to take up arms again. He said: "Defend Kuwait to your last drop of blood."

These clipped words, with their emotive appeal, lifted the morale of all officers and enlisted men who now redeployed without fear in their hearts. Their belief in God was suddenly strengthened, their courage rallied and they resolved there and then to fight to the last for their beloved country. At that moment I felt certain that there was no chance of a surrender. Either a life of freedom and honour or martyrdom for God and country.

▶ Jiwan Camp under attack

At 1000 the bombardment of Jiwan Camp intensified. I took shelter with a comrade in arms behind a screen in the centre of the camp. Neither of us had more than a Colt revolver -- our share of the small arms available. Shrapnel from every direction burst around the position. The sound of artillery, mortars and high explosive charges was ear splitting.

In the first hours of the Jiwan Camp siege, the fusillade concentrated on the headquarters entrance, the Ministry of Defence, the military college and the medical centre. All these structures were hit with heavy Iraqi mortar fire from the north and west. It was clear that all the targets were being struck.

From my position I could see plumes of smoke rising from fires at the military college, the Ministry of Defence and other camp buildings. Structures began to crack asunder from the heavy ordnance directed at Jiwan Camp.

The Iraqi forces attacking Jiwan Camp had concentrated at the Orthology Hospital roundabout not far from the Sulaibikhat neighbourhood and took up positions both inside and outside the Al-Sabah Hospital, after occupying it and evicting the patients. They also deployed much further north in the Doha area with mortars of up to 156mm calibre whose extended range of 20 kilometres could be used to hit targets inside the camp.

The Iraqi invaders could observe their targets from three places around the camp. The first was the dome on the Islamic Medical Cen-

The 156mm howitzer mortar used to attack Jiwan Camp

tre's mosque, the second the Ministry of Electricity & Water's building at Al-Riq'ee and the third was the signals unit building. A platoon of National Guardsmen counter-attacked the Ministry of Electricity & Water and killed the Iraqi officers on the building's roof. In addition to the tell tale marks at the observation post, bullet holes can also be detected at the dome on the Islamic Medical Centre's mosque, giving the lie to suggestions that the Kuwaitis gave in without a fight.

Despite the tremendous odds facing the Kuwaitis -- the surprise attack due to Saddam's deceit, the paltry force of 5,000 Kuwaitis in the camp and the puny weapons available to them, the Kuwaiti army managed with the help of God and the courage of its youth to hold the enemy at bay for more than 10 hours on end. The battle lasted from 0800 until after 1800 before the undefeated Kuwaitis were ordered to retire and abandon their positions.

Ranged against them were more than 120,000 Republican Guards -- the Iraqi dictator's crack troops in terms of weapons, training and morale. They were heavily armed with artillery, tanks, mortars and had a defensive shield from helicopter gunships.

Despite the unequal struggle, unforgettable acts of sacrifice took place:-

● *While the bombardment was at its peak, Lieutenant Ahmed Al-Shammari carried a heavy automatic rifle, regardless of the pain he was suffering from surgery two days earlier. Despite orders from his commanding officer to rest and abandon his post, the gallant officer refused and stayed behind to resist the invaders.*

● *In the battle for Jiwan Camp more than 200 martyrs, most of them raw recruits, were killed in action but only after destroying much of the attacking force's equipment and inflicting heavy losses on the Iraqi troops.*

● *The Iraqi soldiers who attacked our headquarters and the Ministry of Defence were so cowardly that whenever heavy fire was directed at them they hoisted the white flag. When a group of Kuwaiti officers approached them to parley, they opened fire with Kalashnikov AK-47 automatic rifles and artillery. In this way many Kuwaiti personnel were killed.*

● *During the ebb and flow of battle there was good news which raised spirits among the gallant Kuwaiti forces defending Jiwan Camp. H.H. The Amir and the Crown Prince had reached a place of safety outside the country. It was also rumoured that a number of Iraqi soldiers in the Adnan Khairallah Group had staged an attempted coup against Saddam Hussain and had bombed the Presidential Palace in Baghdad.*

● *In a daring counter-attack, Kuwaiti forces captured a Republican Guardsman outside the Ministry of Defence. He was dying from wounds. When a Kuwaiti officer asked him to say the Muslim prayer of the dying, he snarled in an*

16

insulting reference to H.H. The Amir:"I want Jaber, I want Jaber."

● *Earlier at about 1100 Kuwaiti troops captured two senior Iraqi officers -- a colonel and a lieutenant colonel. When searched at the interrogation room, detailed maps were discovered unveiling the whole Iraqi plan for attacking and occupying Kuwait.*

▶ **National Guard stands firm**

The National Guard played a major role in the battle for control of Jiwan Camp. They blocked a huge column of invading tanks which was trying to penetrate Kuwait City via the Fourth Ring Road and forced it to divert to the Fifth and Sixth Ring Roads.

Units of the National Guard were pinned down by heavy Iraqi mortar fire from 0930-2300. They succeeded with the support of a number of Kuwaiti army tanks and by using 50 mm automatic weapons in halting the advance, inflicting hundreds of casualties, especially on the contingent which entered the Police College and tried to break into the National Guard camp.

A friend Captain Dr Waleed Bishara described points in the fight back when wounded men were literally soaked in blood. He managed to save those who were likely to live, with the help of his comrades, doctors and paramedics. After getting the order to evacuate the clinic, he and his colleagues transported the wounded in their own cars rigged out as makeshift ambulances or in a hastily commandeered bus to the

Captain Dr Waleed Bishara of the National Guard

public hospitals at Farwaniya and Addan. The evacuation took place under extremely trying conditions, in the dark and under continuous shelling, so the wounded could be treated or given life saving surgery.

My friend told me: "One of the National Guard officers General Khalid Abdullah Boodai set a great example of sacrifice and patriotism. He returned to the ranks as soon as he heard of the invasion to lead a group of his former military comrades in the Khalidiya area, despite having resigned as director general of the National Guard's Military Commission just a few weeks before the invasion. On rejoining headquarters at Khalidiya he immediately gave orders to return fire with fire. He ordered armoured vehicles to defend H.H. The Amir's Dasman Palace, after a call from the Crown Prince himself and requisitioned

Brigadier Jassim Shehab of the Kuwaiti army to provide a number of tanks as protection for the National Guard camp which was by then under artillery attack. When the Khalidiya area where the headquarters are located was completely surrounded after nightfall on 2 August 1990, General Khalid Boodai was forced, along with his colleagues, to make the toughest decision of his life -- to retreat and evacuate his positions under coordinated incoming fire and with a large number of casualties among the guardsmen."

Colonel Salem Masoud, Commander of the "Martyr Brigade" (formerly 35 Brigade)

General Boodai proved himself a loyal son of Kuwait. He remained in the country throughout the occupation and led one of the most important resistance groups.

▶ *How the invasion began*

The invasion started in the early hours of 2 August 1990. Before mounting a total land, air and sea attack the Iraqis occupied Kuwaiti border posts along the state's northern and western border with Iraq. In a skirmish near Al-Salmi, (Kuwait's western passport centre), a Kuwaiti patrol returned Iraqi fire and killed five enemy soldiers.

The land attack proper led by General Iyad El-Rawi, the Republican Guard Commander, began at 2 a.m. Kuwaiti time when Iraqi forces penetrated the northern border by shelling the passport check point at Abdali. The enemy proceeded to demolish the neighbouring mosque, despite the fact that fighting is prohibited (haram) in that particular month of the year.

The invaders pressed home the advantage of a surprise attack and seized their first objective -- Kuwait's Sixth Brigade -- capturing a number of officers and other ranks before reaching the Al-Mitla Ridge.

The Kuwaiti hero of the hour was Colonel Salem Masoud, commander of 35th Brigade, who rallied his

The Al-Abdali passport control centre north of Kuwait on the southern Iraqi border

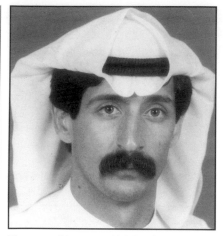

The martyr Lieutenant Abdul Kareem Talib Al-Kandary

troops at the Battle of Josoor Bridge which took place near Al-Mitla. Another hero was Lieutenant Abdul Kareem Talib Al-Kandary. The Lieutenant supported by his gallant unit and five armoured vehicles managed to halt a long convoy of Iraqi tanks, Armoured Personnel Carriers (APCs) and trucks, compelling the enemy to call in an air strike on the Kuwaiti position over a flyover. Lieutenant Al-Kandary was wounded by bullets from Iraqi helicopter gunships and suffered severe burns to his stomach and legs. His comrade in arms Khaled Al-Faylakawi carried him to hospital where he died at 11 a.m. that morning. He was 24 years old. Al-Kandary was married with one son, Youssef, aged two but his wife was pregnant with a second child Badr who was born fatherless in December 1990.

The Kuwaiti Air Force also played a major role in stalling the advance of Iraqi troops in the opening hours of the invasion. Four aircraft took off from the Ali Al-Salem Airbase and straffed the advancing Iraqi tanks inflicting heavy damage before withdrawing, to an airbase in Dhahran, Saudi Arabia.

Major amphibious landings took place from the sea at the Kuwait Towers, the Amiri Hospital and the Seif Palace, under the umbrella of air cover. This attack was pivotal in the Iraqi drive to seize control of H.H. The Amir's residence at Dasman Palace.

▶ *Air attacks on Kuwait*

The Iraqi airforce targeted many important and strategic sites early on 2 August 1990. At 0430 a number of Iraqi fighter bombers straffed the freight runway at Kuwait International Airport. The supervisor Khalil Al-Shatti described how the ground shook under the impact of high explosives. He saw four aircraft dropping bombs east of Terminal 2. The director of civil aviation Shaikh Jaber Mubarak Al-Sabah then ordered him to close the airport to all traffic and to extinguish the runway lights. This prevented the departure of a scheduled British Airways Boeing 747 flight which was about to depart. The Boeing was subsequently destroyed by the Iraqis and the passengers held hostage.

At 0530 an Iraqi jet bombed the communications building at Sabahiya and several storeys collapsed. Later it was totally demolished. The Iraqi airforce also twice hit the Crown Prince's palace overlooking Arabian Gulf Street in the

The martyr Shaikh Fahd Al-Ahmed Al-Sabah

Shaab area between 0600 and 0830 causing heavy damage.

▶ Death of Shaikh Fahd

The younger brother of H.H. The Amir, Shaikh Fahd Al-Ahmed, renowned for his role in the Olympic movement and leadership of the Kuwait Football Federation, was killed defending his country near the western entrance to the Dasman Palace during the early morning of 2 August 1990. He was picked off by a sniper using a high velocity rifle from the old Museum's roof. I saw the white saloon car in which Shaikh Fahd was travelling two days later only 20 metres from the palace's west gate. The car's left hand door was open indicating that Shaikh Fahd got out to return Iraqi fire before he was fatally shot. He was dead on arrival at the Amiri Hospital and buried hurriedly at the Riqqa Cemetery on Saturday 25 August 1990 with a false name on his tomb stone (Abdullah Al-Masri).

According to resistance sources, Iraqi agents tried more than once to discover where he was buried but to no avail. Ali Khalaf Al-Faylakawi was among the dedicated young men who worked in the cemetery throughout the occupation. He suffered greatly from the hardships involved in burying the dead, especially from the constant harassment by Iraqi intelligence officers. He recorded on film many of the martyrs' bodies that were brought for burial. This way vital evidence was collected of Iraqi terrorism. Al-Faylakawi was part of the burial party which laid Shaikh Fahd's body to rest.

Ali Khalaf Al-Faylakawi

▶ Seizing government buildings

A pathfinder group of Iraqi troops and armour reached the heart of Kuwait City at 0300 when gunfire was heard in Fahd Al-Salem Street. Iraqi soldiers beat up passers by and harassed motorists, especially those on their way to work after 0700. The attackers rounded up hundreds of Kuwaitis and expatriates near the Sheraton roundabout and the Orthology Hospital. They rapidly took over key points in Jamal Abdul-Nasser Street in the Shuwaikh area, such as hospitals, the Public Authority of Ports, the Ministry of Communications, the former salt and chlorine factory and the Al-Salam Palace.

After seizing these initial objectives the invading forces deployed in teams, each taking a nominated road where they dug into permanent positions, even if counter-attacked with artillery fire, in line with what soon became obvious was an agreed premeditated plan.

A Kuwaiti cadet on duty at the Bayan Palace on 2 August 1990 found in a captured Iraqi soldier's pocket, a plan giving the route of advance taken by his division from entering Kuwait to reaching the Bayan Palace via the Fifth Ring Road. By following these battle orders, the Iraqis rapidly controlled the Information Ministry Complex, the Seif Palace and the Ministries of Interior and Foreign Affairs.

▶ Control of Police Stations

The occupation forces seized Kuwait's police stations during the course of 4-5 August 1990 in order for them to serve as bases for the Iraqi C.I.D.. Strong resistance was mounted at Keifan district between the Second and Third Ring Roads. The Iraqis were forced to bring up artillery to quell the fightback by surviving Kuwaiti units in that dis-

trict. It took 10 days for the Iraqis to snuff out the last remnants of loyal Kuwaiti forces and the police post itself was ruined.

▶ Radio and Television shutdown

The transmission of Kuwait Radio and Television formally ceased at 0900 on 2 August 1990, after the Iraqis occupied the Ministry of Information Complex. While I was on duty at Jiwan Camp, however, I saw Kuwait Television broadcasting patriotic songs and a still photo of H.H. The Amir and the Crown Prince. The picture was blurred indicating that the broadcast was coming from a studio outside the Ministry of Information or from one of the mobile broadcast units.

The Voice of Kuwait Radio was also interrupted but a band of loyal Kuwaitis managed with make shift equipment to restore the transmission for 10 continuous days before Iraqi agents found the broadcast site. They moved their equipment from one place to another, taking grave risks. First they based themselves at the Dasma Studio until Friday 3 August 1990. They then shifted to Tawfic Al Ameer's home in the Sabah Al-Salem district. Finally they moved to the Shaikh Mohamed Yousif Al-Saud Al-Sabah Palace in Salwa but on 12 August 1990 the transmission finally went off the air with these dramatic words: "Arabs, brothers, beloved brothers, Muslims. Hurry to our aid..."

The radio team comprised a number of technicians and radio journalists. Among them were

Tawfic Al-Ameer

The damaged Umm Al-Aish earth satellite station in the Rawdatain area

Mansour Al-Mansour, Salwa Hussain, Mahmood Saqr, Yousuf Mostafa, Ali Hassan, Hameed Khaja, Abdul Aziz Al-Mansour, Engineer Samir Abu Ghosh, Azwar Yaseen, Advocate Abdullah Al-Ayoub, Fadel Maarafi, Abdul Aziz Al-Baghli, Dr Abdul Aziz Al-Saqr, Tawfic Al-Ameer, Hussain Al-Mansour, Ali and Ibrahim Al-Ameer and Walid Al-Ayoub.

▶ *Communications are cut*

It was 2200 on Saturday 4 August 1990 when large areas of Kuwait were cut off from the outside world. The Iraqis had destroyed the Umm Al Aish earth satellite station in northern Kuwait and interrupted the communications channels from microwave transmitters in the downtown.

Communications inside Kuwait were maintained except in certain areas including Hadiya, Sabahiya, Rikka and Ahmadi. They were finally cut in all areas of Kuwait on 7 February 1991, possibly because the Iraqis feared intelligence would be passed to the allies. Mobile phones belonging to the mobile communications company were terminated on 18 August 1990.

Resistance fighters maintained links with the outside world right up to the liberation. Vital information about the Iraqis military machine and their preparations was filtered out of the country. Among those who risked their lives transmitting from secret satellite phones were Shaikh Sabah Nasser Al-Saud Al-Sabah, Shaikh Ali Salem Al-Ali, Shaikh Athbi Fahd Al-Ahmed, General Khalid Boodai, Colonel Fahd Al Ameer, Nasser Al-Farsi, Captain

The martyr Asrar Al-Qabandi - the first woman to contact CNN from occupied Kuwait

22

Ama'ar Al-Ajmi and the martyred Asrar Al-Qabandi.

▶ *Nationals seek Saudi refuge*

The residents of Jahra and Sulaibikhat townships were introduced to the cruelty of the invading forces early on 2 August 1990. People awoke in horror at the sound of artillery fire, small arms and tank tracks. Storm troopers entered the private homes of unarmed civilians, abused them, stole gold and money and subjected women to bestial rape. They also demanded food to eat on the spot.

It was a day of shame and humiliation. Some women fled in their nightclothes carrying children in their arms to escape the rapacious horde. Saddam's soldiers stopped at nothing to put their mark on Kuwait. They entered the nurses homes in the Riq'ee area opposite Jiwan Camp and raped women of various nationalities. They then evicted sick children and old people from hospital beds.

News of these atrocities spread rapidly and many Kuwaitis, fearing the worst, fled to Saudi Arabia with their belongings. Sadly many families taking overland routes to the kingdom through the desert died from exposure and dehydration before reaching safety. Those who arrived in Saudi Arabia were well looked after by their temporary hosts in the true spirit of Arab hospitality.

▶ *Enter the Iraqi settlers*

After the invasion, thousands of Iraqi settlers or "makhakirah" from Basra and the southern Iraqi villages entered Kuwait. The carpetbaggers arrived in the first days after the invasion, often barefoot carrying small Primus stoves and wandering the streets of the capital. Decent people were appalled at the sight of these uncouth country louts defecating in the open and throwing garbage everywhere.

A friend witnessed a family of "makhakirah" helping themselves to goods from Al-Muthanna Complex. He saw a man with 10 wristwatches on each arm. When he reported the theft he realised that the soldiers were watching the complex to protect the thieves.

▶ *Postscript -- Arabian Gulf Street*

On the evening of Saturday 4 August I saw Iraqi tanks in Arabian Gulf Street stretching in a continuous line from Kuwait Towers until the end of the Bidaa Road near the Messila Beach Hotel. The road was clogged with mud from the tank tracks. Its pavements were cracked by the weight of enemy equipment. Iraqi soldiers were washing their clothes in sea water while others begged for food and cigarettes. In the early dawn of Sunday 5 August 1990 the tanks seized the Fahaheel Expressway and the Sixth Ring Road but curiously the Baghdad government had announced its intention to mount an orderly withdrawal, with effect from later that day. It was a cruel deception -- for this indeed was Kuwait's darkest hour.

FROM QUISLING REGIME TO ANNEXATION

From the first day of the Iraqi invasion to 28 August 1990 the Ba'athist regime in Baghdad issued a series of resolutions aimed at erasing the name of Kuwait from the political map. The only people likely to believe them, however, were the Iraqis who had lived under Saddam Hussein's repressive rule for more than 20 years.

The Baghdad government declared on 2 August 1990 that the Kuwaiti Government "has fallen as a result of an internal revolution in Kuwait." Kuwaiti citizens were surprised to see invasion forces waving "V for Victory" signs at them in the streets. When questioned, Iraqi soldiers told them: "We came to save you and to support the popular revolution."

The Iraqi dictator had attempted to exploit all the circumstances surrounding Kuwait's National Council elections in June 1990. He invited certain Kuwaiti nationals who had opposed the elections to attend the Baghdad celebrations to mark the July anniversary of the Ba'athist Revolution.

His plot failed since the opposition leaders, despite their differences with the government in Kuwait, would not surrender a single clod of earth from their motherland as a price for their support for Saddam Hussein's political charade.

It is worth remembering at this point that the occupation forces were denied their initial goal when H.H. The Amir and members of his cabinet left for Saudi Arabia. This cup was made doubly bitter by the passage at the U.N. Security Council of Resolution 660 in which the Iraqi invasion was condemned by a majority vote and Iraq was instructed to withdraw from the state and instigate negotiations with Kuwait.

Nevertheless, from the occupied Ministry of Information Complex came transmissions on television of a so called Provisional Free Kuwait Government with announcements declaring:" All the people are in support of the Leader Alaa Hussain Ali."

The "government" comprised the following:

Waleed Saud Mohamed - Minister of Foreign Affairs

Saad Hussain Ahmed--Minister of Finance & Oil

Hussain Ali Dheiman--Minister of Social Affairs, Works and Public Works

Fadel Haider Al-Wafaiki--Minister of Information and Communications

Misha'al Saad Al-Hadab--Minister of Housing Affairs

Nasser Mansour Al-Mandeel--Minister of Higher Education

Essam Abdul Majeed Hussain--Minister of Justice, Legal Affairs, Endowments and Islamic Affairs

Yacoub Mohamed Shallal--Minister of Commerce, Electricity & Planning.

It soon became obvious from interviews on Baghdad television that these men had been forced to make statements under duress. Most of them were military men who had been seized at Orthology Roundabout or at other army sites on the first day of the invasion.

The news of this short-lived quisling regime was received with derision. Young Kuwaiti men and women wrote graffiti on the walls such as "Allauddine and the Magic Lamp" and "Alaa - Soap awaits you in the market." The occupation forces reacted angrily to this defiance. Graffiti artists were arrested and punished either by arson at their homes or execution of the householder.

Kuwait's quisling, an accountant by profession, was born in 1959 and married with two children Saad and Huda. His wife was arrested 13 days after the provisional government was formed. Ali took a B.Sc. in accountancy at Baghdad University in 1982 and before the invasion had been working as financial controller of a company specialising in making cardboard at the Sabhan Industrial Area.

His parents and brothers (he was the eldest in the family) were surprised to see him appear on television as the "President" of a provisional government. His father said his son was arrested between Al Fardaws and Al Andalus on the first morning of the invasion while intending to join his unit at Jiwan Camp.

▶ *The "Kuwaiti Republic"*

Saddam Hussain continued with this tragic farce. He changed the "Provisional Free Kuwait Government" into the "Kuwait Republic". It was the next step to annexing Kuwait to Iraq. The Kuwait Republic must have been one of the shortest lived governments in history since it only lasted 30 hours.

The only event of note during the Provisional Free Government was Saddam Hussain's statement that Iraqi forces would withdraw from Kuwait in an orderly fashion from the morning of Sunday 5 August 1990. Television crews showed columns of trucks, tanks and Armoured Personnel Carriers (APCs) leaving Kuwait for Iraq where the women of Basra received them as "heroes" with songs and garlands of flowers.

The international news media exposed this chicanery. American spy satellites confirmed with shots taken on 4 August 1990 that far from withdrawing the Iraqis had reinforced their invasion bridgehead. Military vehicles were seen moving south towards Saudi Arabia's northern borders following the Fahaheel Expressway and Al-Safr Motorway.

▶ *The annexation of Kuwait*

On Wednesday 8 August 1990 the Iraqi Revolution Command Council issued a resolution purporting to annexe Kuwait officially to Iraq, designating it the 19th governorate. Kuwait City was renamed Kazimah. Iraqi Television showed members of the Provisional Free Kuwait Government meeting Saddam Hussain and his deputy Izzat Ibrahim al-Doori and offering amalgamation to the Iraqi regime. The Iraqi leader rewarded the quislings, whom he claimed had asked for unity with Iraq, by issuing a republican decree appointing them as advisers in the Prime Minister's Office and ministers of state. Saddam Hussain claimed in the media that Kuwait had never been a real country but was part of Iraq detached by "British imperialism." He asked: "Is it reasonable that a country like Iraq with a civilisation of more than 6,000 years should have no sea window on the Gulf."

In reality, Iraq had recognised Kuwait as a free independent sovereign state under an agreement signed on Friday 4 October 1963, a copy of which was filed with the United Nations. The Kuwaiti delegation which signed the agreement comprised - the late Shaikh Sabah Al-Salem Al-Sabah, then Crown Prince; H.H. Shaikh Saad Al-Abdullah Al-Salem, then Minister of the Interior and acting Foreign Minister; the late Khalifah Khalid Al-Ghunaim, Minister of Commerce and adviser Abdul Rahman Salem Al-Ateeqi, Deputy minister of Foreign Affairs. The Iraqi signatories were the then Vice-president Ahmed Hassan Al-Bakr and Defence Minister Saleh Mahdi Ammash.

Events showed that Saddam Hussain betrayed this pact, as well as his telephone pledges on 1 August 1990 to Saudi Arabia's King Fahd and Egypt's President Mubarak that he would not use force against Kuwait. To complete the final act of his annexation comedy, Saddam Hussain invited a troupe of drummers from the "makhakirah" who were used at Al-Rihab Complex in Tunis Street at Hawalli and on the Corniche at Shaab. They raised placards and shouted slogans of support for the annexation.

Baghdad Television broadcast an interview with Kuwaiti ambassador to Iraq Ibrahim Al-Bah'hoo and Shaikh Salem Fahd Al-Salem Al-Sabah, after their arrest. They were forced under duress to praise Saddam Hussain and support the return of "the branch to the root."

The United Nations Security Council was not duped by these moves. On Thursday 9 August 1990 Resolution 662 was passed cancelling the annexation of Kuwait by Iraq as null and void and denying Saddam Hussain's declaration of 6 August 1990 that his occupation of Kuwait was permanent.

▶ *The 19th Governorate*

On 28 August 1990 Saddam Hussain officially amalgamated Kuwait into

26

Shaikh Ahmed Al-Qattan - the first person to expose the atrocities committed in occupied Kuwait by the Iraqi military governor Ali Hassan Al-Majeed

Iraq as the 19th governorate. These were difficult days for Kuwaitis. Many citizens were filled with apprehension when Saddam Hussain appointed his cousin Ali Hassan Al-Majeed as military governor of Kuwait. The latter earned a reputation for genocide when he ordered the deaths of 4,000 Kurdish villagers in the Halabja area of Iraq in 1988 using chemical weapons. Fears grew after a speech by Shaikh Ahmed Al-Qattan who gave graphic details of the atrocities committed by Al-Majeed. His unique brutality, aided by Sab'awi Ibrahim and other evil Iraqi C.I.D. men, spread terror for all 208 days of the occupation.

▶ *12 August initiative*

Kuwaitis, being trapped in their own country, were susceptible to sudden glimmers of hope that the nightmare would end. The first false dawn was the withdrawal deception on 5 August 1990. The second letdown was when the Arab states divided at the Arab League summit in Cairo on 10 August 1990. No firm resolution to expel the Iraqis from Kuwait was adopted. Iraq then declared an important initiative for Sunday 12 August 1990. The Ba'athist radio announcer Murad Maqdad, who only read communiques from "the tyrant", produced another disappointment. The 12 August initiative simply linked any withdrawal from Kuwait to a solution of the intractable Palestinian problem.

Hopes were raised three days later when a second "initiative" was promised but Maqdad only declared that Saddam Hussain had agreed to Iran's conditions for settling the 1980-88 Iran-Iraq war.

Saddam's initiative backfired. This was the man who signed the 1975 agreement with the Shah of Iran in Algiers in 1975 over the Shatt Al-Arab and then shredded it before television cameras, unleashing an eight-year war that ended in the deaths of 1 million people. Thirty brigades of his forces withdrew from the Iranian border on 17 August 1990 in support of the 150,000 in Kuwait but the Islamic Republic of Iran was not fooled. This was no Stalin-Hitler pact, for the Iranians remained neutral during the Kuwait liberation war. They failed to join Saddam's cause, remembering the blood on his hands and insisted instead that Iraq should quit Kuwait.

Plate 16. An Iraqi tank attacked by Kuwaiti resistance fighters bearing slogans condemning the so called Provisional Free Kuwait Government

Plate 17. Ibrahim Al-Bah'oo - Kuwait's ambassador in Baghdad before the invasion

Plate 18. The leader of the so called Provisional Free Kuwait Government Ala'a Hussain Ali with his two children Saad and Huda

Plate 19. A slogan written by Kuwaitis condemning the so called Provisional Free Kuwait Government

Plate 20. The names were changed on the plates but not in reality - see the yellow writing

Plate 21. A chalet in the Bneider area with an Iraqi slogan claiming Kuwait as a governorate and part of Iraq

Plate 22. A burned corpse with evidence of torture to the legs done by a sharp knife - the author found in Damascus Street, Surra, on 28 February 1991.

Plate 22. A burned corpse with evidence of torture to the legs done by a sharp knife - the author found in Damascus Street, Surra, on 28 February 1991.

Plate 23. Sulphuric acid was used to disfigure this body

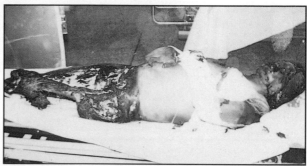

Plate 24. The eyes were gouged out with an iron probe

Plate 25. Iraqi CID men were guarded by special forces during house to house searches

Plate 26. This Kuwaiti home at Rawda was burned as a reprisal because an Iraqi soldier was found killed in a nearby park

Plate 27. The Iraqi slogan boasts that "special forces men are the ones for difficult missions" but it should have added " they are the ones for stealing missions as well"

Plate 28.Iraqi dinar notes used during the occupation

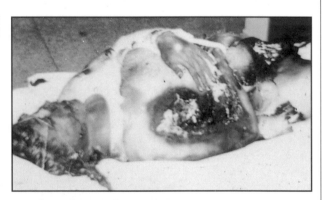

Plate 29. A Kuwaiti dinar note cancelled after Iraqi troops looted the Central Bank strongroom

Plate 30. A body tortured with burns and acid

Plate 31. The palace belonging to the late Shaikh Mubarak Abdullah Al-Jaber used as a torture centre

REIGN OF TERROR IN KUWAIT

In the name of God, the Benevolent, the Merciful

And surely we shall try you with something of fear and hunger and loss of wealth and lives and crops but give glad tidings to the steadfast

Who say, when a misfortune striketh them: Lo! we are Allah's and lo unto him we are returning

Holy Quran
The Cow Surah (155-156)

Saddam Hussain's reign of terror in Kuwait started on the first day of the occupation. Thousands of Kuwaiti men and women including youths and children were tortured. Some were permanently disabled or executed. There is scarcely a family in Kuwait who did not share in the terror and misery exacted on innocent people by the Iraqi C.I.D. What follows in this chapter is only a sample of the atrocities committed by the invaders.

▶ *Shooting at peaceful protesters*

Kuwaitis doubted the Iraqi claims that an "internal insurrection" or "popular revolution" had taken place. From the second day of the invasion men, women and children came out onto the streets in all parts of the city, brandishing banners condemning the invasion and carrying patriotic portraits of H.H. The Amir and H.H. The Crown Prince.

The demonstrations were spontaneous -- a true expression of the depth of revulsion at the Iraqis among ordinary citizens. The invaders were shocked and some of the soldiers who believed their own propaganda expressed surprise. Military governor Ali Hassan Al-Majeed issued instructions to his Special Forces to

Found in a house at Mishrif on 25 August 1990 - see how the face has been tortured

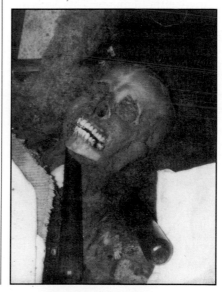

Demonstrations broke out all over Kuwait condemning the occupation and demanding unity in the face of the aggressor

suppress all demonstrations by firing over the heads of marchers. The first warning shots were fired at Rumaithiya park. This soon changed to firing indiscriminately into the crowd without mercy. This occurred during the women's demonstration starting in Al-Jaberiya area near the Mubarak Al-Kabir Hospital. One victim was a Kuwaiti girl from the Al-Foderi family.

Chemistry student Sana'a Abdul-Rahman Al-Foderi was among the first of the Kuwaiti women martyrs. She joined demonstrations against the occupation in which unarmed civilians carried portraits of the Amir and Crown Prince. Sana'a showed unforgettable courage in continuing with the protest with about 20 other women after others had fled. Her last words while lying bleeding in her mother's arms were:" My role has ended...Take care of my brother Fahd." She died at 6.30 p.m. on 8 August 1990 after being shot by an

The martyr Sana'a Al-Foderi - the first woman killed in a peaceful demonstration

officer trying to disperse protesters at Al-Jaberiya Police Station. Sana'a died before reaching the Mubarak Al-Kabir Hospital. Her murderer took pleasure in pumping several shots into her defenceless body.

▶ *Evicting hospital patients*

The invasion troops brought with them a medical team of Iraqi doctors to control and administer hospitals. Their tasks included preparing inventories of equipment to be removed to Iraq and to spy on Kuwaiti and expatriate medics. One of the Directorate-General of Health in the Governorate of Kuwait's first directives was to evacuate from all hospitals 80% of the sick to receive military casualties. Thereafter, "cold cases" were not allowed as in-patients and many of the sick, especially those receiving treatment at specialised centres, were obliged to vacate their beds. The clear-out particularly affected the Hussain Makki Centre for Cancer Treatment, the Sabah Hospital's Electrodialysis Centre and the Mubarak Al-Kabir Hospital.

The director of the Mubarak Al-Kabir Hospital Dr Yousef Ahmed Al-Nisf continued with his job from the first day of the invasion. He recalls:" We implemented an emergency plan at dawn on 2 August 1990 after getting a message about the Iraqi attack. We admitted about 150 wounded people on the first day, most of whom were Kuwaiti military personnel injured in the Iraqi assault on Jiwan Camp. Our first Kuwaiti casualty at 0430 hrs was a young Kuwaiti man shot in the shoulder near the Minister of Information complex. Fifteen minutes later we admitted a Kuwaiti officer from the Interior Ministry who had been shot through the left thigh while on his way to work. The bleeding was severe and his life could not be saved in time due to his rare blood group.

" Ambulances started arriving at our gates after 0900 hrs. We admitted wounded Iraqi soldiers, one of whom was the pilot of a helicopter that crashed in Hawali. He was severely burned but we did our duty as doctors.

" We also treated the leader of the attack on Jiwan Camp -- a Lieutenant-Colonel Taha Mahmoud who was badly wounded. He had been shot in the knee during an assault on the Jiwan Camp gate. His leg had to be amputated and he remained in hospital for seven days. This particular officer was brought to hospital by a Kuwaiti ambulance.

" On Saturday 10 August the Iraqi forces took control of the hospital. It was surrounded by soldiers under a lieutenant-colonel who bullied and harassed our staff until stopped by the wounded Iraqi officer who told of the humane treatment he had received at our hands. The wounded Iraqis were transferred out of the hospital in stolen buses but the other injured were simply loaded into the vehicles without consideration of their injuries. I protested about the manhandling.

"Two days later I was surprised to find three Iraqi doctors in my office -- Dr Hussain Mortadha Al-Hakim, a consultant surgeon and director of Baghdad Hospital and two colleagues. They told me they had a letter from Baghdad ordering them to work in the hospital. I was to meet a "Director of Kuwait Health", Dr Abdul Jabbar Abdul Abbas, who I found sitting at the Minister of Health's desk in Al-Sharq.

"I received a political lecture on the return of the branch to the root and was warned to accept this as a reality. I was told that doctors' salaries would be unchanged on the orders of the Iraqi Revolution Command Council. After that I stayed in the hospital for seven days without going home.

When Dr Mortadha got no co-operation from staff, he had to control the hospital by force with the help of a colonel who was also an orthopaedic surgeon. An intelligence officer was also put in post to maintain security and changed every three weeks, together with a 45-strong team from the militia who controlled entry and exit points. Any wounded Kuwaiti was spied upon.

"Among the martyrs who we were unable to save because of the severity of their injuries was Lieutenant Qoushai'an Al-Motairi who suffered stomach wounds in the assault on Jiwan Camp.

"Although there is no maternity wing at the Mubarak Hospital Dr Adnan Al-Shatti, a psychology lecturer in Kuwait University, suggested that his wife Dr Iman Al-Motawa'a take charge of pregnant mothers. The third wing was used for this after smuggling in equipment from elsewhere. The number of women doctors reached 35, all of them Kuwaiti, and they were helped by the martyr Dr Hisham Al-Obaidan. The wing was closed on 1 November 1990 after bringing 725 babies into the world.

"The Iraqis issued an absurd order restricting medicine to three day rations and to accident victims. I met with a number of colleagues during the occupation and we met together to organise work within the hospitals.

"As for rape cases" Dr Al-Nisf added, "we received six of them, two of whom were Palestinian women. All were in a very bad physical condition because of the brutal and barbaric attacks they had endured from Iraqi soldiers.

"After the allied air attacks began we received wounded Iraqi military personnel. One told me the trenches made for their protection were inadequate as soldiers were buried alive due to the heavy bombing," Dr Al-Nisf said.

In a separate incident a friend of the author's elderly father was being treated for a fractured foot at Al-Razi Hospital. Iraqi soldiers kicked him viciously in front of his terrified family and booted him from his bed.

Maternity hospitals were not spared. Women who were booked in for normal deliveries were not allowed to stay more than five hours on the ward. A friend's wife was brutally thrown out of bed into a wheelchair without any privacy with

Dr Yousef Al-Nisf - director-general of the Hawalli medical area

her garments still wet with blood from childbirth.

Iraqi military personnel received absolute priority for treatment in Kuwaiti hospitals, whether for medicine or access to beds. Kuwaitis were kept waiting. Among the victims was the former governor of Hawalli Abdul Latif Al-Berjis who died from a heart attack which could not be treated in time.

I watched as my own father-in-law died slowly at the Mubarak Al-Kabir Hospital due to medical neglect and shortage of staff and equipment. In the whole ward, there was only one heart monitor and that was out of order.

One Iraqi doctor at Al-Addan hospital told a Kuwaiti friend who he had begun to trust: "You Kuwaitis have got tired of Saddam Hussain after two months. How about us? We have lived under him for more than 20 years?"

The entrances to the hospitals were naturally guarded but the Iraqis also planted agents in the treatment rooms to maintain full control of admissions and spot any resistance fighters who might be there for treatment.

A doctor who worked in the Intensive Care Unit at Al-Addan Hospital describes a revealing incident: "The Iraqi C.I.D. brought in a young Kuwaiti with a bullet wound in the head. Part of his scalp was missing. The C.I.D. men insisted hysterically that every effort must be made to keep him alive until the interrogation could be completed." They were denied the information they sought. A few minutes later the boy died.

▶ *Paradise for car thieves*

The Iraqi officers and men who invaded Kuwait had no respect for the private property of either citizens or expatriates. They took cars like common thieves at gun point and sometimes by stopping motorists and kicking them out of their vehicles. A young man was evicted from his Mercedes by force at Jamal Abdul-Nasser Street in Shuwaikh. When he had refused to budge they threatened to kill him saying, "we are not taking the car for ourselves, it is required for our commander." The commander was waiting on the opposite pavement for the car he coveted and the proxy thief got what he wanted.

Special Forces troops who controlled the checkpoints at the start of the crisis specialised in seizing pick-ups, 4X4 vehicles and mini-buses to use on manoeuvres in Kuwait, since their own antiquated Russian equipment was falling to pieces with age. The barefaced cheek of the Iraqi troops led them to repaint stolen vehicles in desert camouflage in an attempt to cover up their crimes.

▶ God is Great -- strikes terror

The next collective act of resistance to the Iraqis was planned for 11 August 1990. Kuwaitis agreed between them, through secretly distributed circulars and telephone calls, to climb onto their roofs at midnight on that day and shout the call to prayer -- Allah Akbar (God is Great).

At the specified time the shouts went out from men, women and children alike, together with loyal slogans about the Amir. The noise continued for 30 minutes frightening the wits out of Iraqis manning checkpoints. The soldiers believed a clandestine organisation was behind this protest. When the next agreed time for this unique act of civil disobedience came on Saturday 1 September 1990 and the shouting of Allah Akbar rang out the Iraqis were so frightened that they fired small arms, rocket propelled grenades and hand-grenades wildly into the night.

The repression was carried a stage further when APCs were dispatched to residential areas and militiamen fired their Kalashnikov AK-47s at the houses were Kuwaitis were shouting "Allah Akbar." An incident of this was reported at Block 12 in Al-Rumaithiya district.

▶ Terrorist circulars

The Iraqi C.I.D. men printed newsletters and distributed them to shoppers as they left the co-operative supermarkets. Kuwaitis who refused to accept them were put under surveillance by the secret police. I was handed a circular on 12 September 1990 at a co-operative in Hawalli. There were 10 orders in all, to be complied with by Sunday 16 September 1990, five of which were the following:

- *All military servants from the Ministries of Interior and Defence -- the National Guard was omitted -- to report for work.*

- *Kuwaitis to surrender their weapons. Those found with guns shall be liable to execution.*

- *Any house from where shots are fired will be demolished together with surrounding properties in a radius of 360 degrees.*

- *Civil servants failing to report for work will be sacked in accordance with a Revolution Command Council instruction.*

- *All Kuwaitis must take their vehicles to the Basra Traffic Department for new number plates or their vehicles will be confiscated.*

This circular caused new fear in the

hearts of many nationals and was the start of a brutal campaign of repression which lasted for many months.

▶ *House searches*

The only circumstances in which a Kuwaiti home can be lawfully searched is on the authority of a warrant issued by the Attorney General. The Iraqis made housebreaking a common practice. Most Kuwaiti districts were thoroughly searched after the third week in September 1990 with Salmiya the first to go.

Few residents were aware of the searches until they were happening. Early morning was a favourite time. During the curfew hours, a sudden cordon sanitaire would be thrown round an area but Kuwaitis would defy this by tipping each other off by telephone once the search parties arrived in a neighbourhood.

Top of the hit list were Kuwaiti VIPs, members of the Kuwaiti army, police or National Guard, as well as weapons and ammunition. Other items which attracted attention were quantities of Kuwaiti currency, portraits of H.H. The Amir and H.H. The Crown Prince, Kuwaiti flags, cassettes of patriotic songs, circulars from the resistance, video cameras, facsimile machines and photocopiers. The searches were aimed at lowering morale and breaking the back of the resistance.

Many Kuwaitis suffered from the erratic and unpredictable behaviour of these search parties. At dawn on Saturday 24 November 1990 the area around my home was surrounded from every side by the Iraqi militia. Soldiers stood not more than 20 metres apart carrying automatic weapons.

At 0700 there was a loud knocking on my front door. I opened up and was confronted by three armed civilians. They were Iraqi C.I.D. officers, backed up by an officer in a lieutenant's uniform and about 23 Special Forces troops armed with AK-47s and RPGs. They deployed rapidly all over my house. The C.I.D. men made a thorough and professional search of every room, rifling through drawers, desks, even a personal telephone book. Clothing was scattered piece after piece. Children's toys were not spared. Furniture was removed from its fixtures and pictures taken down from the walls.

During the search I was asked for my place of work and civil I.D. card but as a double check they asked my child where I worked to see if I was a military man. I held my nerve during this search and clung to my faith in God for deliverance. I was most afraid when they entered one of my private rooms, because I knew there were many incriminating things there, even one of which would be enough to have me executed.

The search was sudden. There had not been enough time to hide anything but the Iraqis had got what they wanted -- a mobile telephone, a facsimile machine, a photocopier, a video recorder and a pocket dictaphone. Owning a photocopier was punishable by death since the machine could be used to print resistance newsletters. One of the Iraqis asked me nervously: "What do you use these items for?" I answered: "They are for my personal use and fit in with what I do for a living." I showed him the invoices for each item.

The Iraqi was unconvinced. All the items were ordered to be confiscated and were recorded on a piece of paper. I was told to report to General Headquarters in a week's time. The blood was pounding through my veins but the visit was not yet over. One of the C.I.D. officers, called Kazim, was leafing through a prayer book called "Heritage". Between two of the pages was a leaflet from the resistance denouncing the occupation. I could only thank God when Kazim returned the book to me without noticing the circular. It was my second deliverance -- the first having come during the shelling at Jiwan Camp.

▶*Arbitrary Arrests*

Random arrests of men or women by day or night was a favoured tactic of the Iraqi C.I.D.. Advocate Abdullah Al-Ayoub was accused in front of his own children with resistance activities and was threatened with execution. The C.I.D. used police stations as prisons and soon these were overcrowded with the accused unable to sleep or even sit on the floor. Schools were then turned into detention centres, guarded by militiamen and Special Forces troops.

The Iraqis fabricated many reasons for detaining people. A group of young Kuwaiti men undertook distribution and home delivery of food in Rumaithiya after the Iraqis tried to seize all supplies of tea, sugar, rice and flour at the co-operative society's warehouses. The C.I.D. arrested these philantrophists in November 1990 and accused them of "damaging the national economy." A group of other youths who enquired about their whereabouts were also pulled in for questioning. All are still missing.

The Iraqi police were especially on the watch for young men distributing resistance newsletters and for Kuwaiti doctors treating resistance casualties.

Many Kuwaitis paid for their patriotism with their lives. Mahmoud

The martyr Mahmoud K. Al-Jassim - the first man killed while distributing a clandestine newsletter condemning the occupation

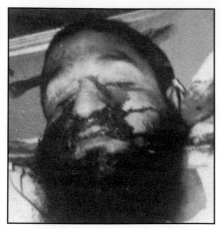

The martyr Mahmoud Al-Jassim after being tortured

Khalifa Al-Jassim, married with five children, was one of the martyrs who endured every kind of torture, after being accused of distributing resistance leaflets. He was found murdered with torture marks on his face near the Yarmouk Club in Mishrif district.

One of his friends who lived with him in the Salmiya district said of his comrade: "The late Mahmoud Khalifa wanted to give his life for God's cause. When Saddam's soldiers invaded he was unable to rest and continually urged me to follow him and kill the Iraqis and make every effort to resist the enemy. He was distributing a newsletter called Sawt Al-Haq (Voice of Truth) at the time he was arrested at the end of August 1990."

The Iraqis apparently believe that crime is a "family affair" -- a notion confirmed by the well known Iraqi journalist Hassan Al-Alawi in an interview with Qatari Television. The principle was enacted on members of a Kuwaiti family all of whom were arrested at 0800 on Wednesday 14 November 1990, because their 19-year-old son Ahmed had taken part in the resistance against the

A Kuwaiti family who were subjected to psychological torture for more than three months

The martyr Dr Hisham Al-Obaidan

The martyr Mubarak Falih Al-Noot

Iraqis. His family was told they would all go home in a few hours after signing a statement that Ahmed would cease contact with the resistance. It was a cruel trick. The family of Abdul-Rahman Al-Rifai were only allowed home 116 days later on 9 March 1991, after being freed by Islamic revolution guerrillas in Iraq, the confirmation for which I owe to Mrs Latifa Al-Rashid Al-Badr.

I later met this family who had been subjected to months of psychological torture and thought they would die in the heavy allied bombardment unleashed on Iraq's towns and cities. They told me that at least five other Kuwaiti families, with children, had been jailed for four months at Basra and Diwania, suffering from fear, hunger and the brutality of their captors. Among

them were the relatives of Safar Ma'rafi, Ahmed Matar, Ahmed Al-Musaileim, Maatook Al-Fulaij and Abdul Wahab Bin Hussain Al-Roomi.

These families endured the Iraqi winter wearing the same summer clothes they stood up in when transported from Kuwait. They suffered constant hunger and thirst. Their diet was confined to maize, bread and foul water which caused diarrhoea. Their beds were filthy cement floors open at all times to the elements.

Al-Rifa'i family was held without charge for 48 days in the Security Department at Basra. It was simply a frightening tactic. The father of the family was placed in a separate jail but lost contact with his son Ahmed. The son's present whereabouts are unknown. The rest of the family is

Member of Parliament Dr Khalid Al-Wasmi   *Captain Khalil Al-Saleh - a Kuwait Airways pilot*

reunited in free Kuwait but is still awaiting Ahmed's return.

▶ Martyrs from all classes

Kuwaitis from all walks of life gave their lives during the occupation. Dr Hisham Al-Obaidan, a colleague of mine in the 16th Officer Group, was executed by the Iraqis charged with treating wounded members of the resistance. Mubarak Al-Noot, general manager of the Ardiya Co-operative Society, was another hero. He refused to hang portraits of the Iraqi President in place of the Amir and Crown Prince's pictures on the walls of his administrative office. Because of this act of defiance he was blindfolded and publicly executed by two bullets through the head outside the co-op.

Another story of heroism is that of Captain Khalil Ibrahim Al-Saleh, aged 33, a Kuwait Airways Corporation pilot. He was arrested on Sunday 25 November 1990 and accused of distributing money to Kuwaiti families, members of the resistance and military men. Saleh, together with a number of colleagues including Fahd Al-Baghli, hid the captain and flight crew of the British Airways Boeing 747, which was trapped at Kuwait International Airport on the day of the invasion, at a house in Rumaithiya and kept them there until his arrest.

Saleh was punished with 57 days detention in Kuwait before being deported to Al-Hartha Prison at Basra and after that to a detention camp at Diwania in the Qadisiyya Governorate. He was cruelly beaten with whips, electric wires and batons while his hands were trussed like a chicken and his eyes blindfolded. Bursts of electrical power were applied to sensitive areas of his body and his feet were scorched in several places.

Captain Saleh says: "When the C.I.D. men discovered after a period of torture that I was a pilot, they changed their approach to me and demanded that I work for Iraqi Airways and that I carried arms against the Americans." Iraqi pilots working for the airline were implicated in the theft of eight Airbuses owned by Kuwait Airways by flying the stolen aircraft to Baghdad.

Saleh recalls other memories of torture. He says: "I saw plain clothes policemen ripping out the finger nails of young men who had been arrested. One was tied by his feet to a butcher's meat hook. His head hung down but he was left suspended for more than 30 minutes. Another youth defied the C.I.D. at Nayif Palace. While he was being tortured he shouted,' by God even if Saddam Hussain came here now, I would kill him.' I have no idea of his fate."

Captain Saleh was freed by Muslim rebels on 9 March 1991 after they broke into his detention camp during their abortive uprising against Saddam Hussain. He arrived home with other Kuwaiti detainees on 17 March 1991.

These are only a few examples of Iraqi atrocities. The invaders turned the whole country into a prison. Even sports clubs were used for these crimes. As residents of Edailiyah know full well, they would hear the screams of men and women undergoing torture every night at the Kazima Sports Club.

▶ *Denuding Failaka Island*

The archaeologically rich Failaka Island was seized by the Iraqis in the first days of the occupation. The invaders tried every means possible to expel the population by requisitioning all food and provisions from homes and shops. Families were forced to pay extortionate amounts of up to 1,000 Iraqi Dinars to transport themselves and their belongings by ferry from Failaka harbour to Ras Al- Ard in Salmiya. The island was deserted for the first time in thousands of years but four people managed to remain -- two in hiding and two by lying to the Iraqis.

The telegraph office at Failaka Island - damaged by bombing

► *Currency theft -- in broad daylight*

Kuwaiti currency was literally stolen in broad daylight on the orders of the Iraqi authorities. The Revolution Command Council ruled on 24 September 1990 that the Kuwaiti Dinar (KD) was no longer legal tender and would be withdrawn from circulation from Saturday 6 October 1990. The KD could be exchanged for the Iraqi currency at par.

Kuwaitis were unimpressed by Saddam Hussein's claim that the Kuwaiti Government had forced down the value of the Iraqi dinar to 1/25th of the KD. In reality, of course, the once rich Iraqi economy had collapsed because of Saddam Hussein's wars, his military expenditure and wasteful extravagance, as well as his support for international terrorism.

Some nationals continued to deal only in KD after 6 October 1990 but were later compelled to hide their supplies away or exchange some of them for Iraqi money. The attempt at equalising the two currencies, however, was a failure. An active black market sprang up at Salwa and Bneid Al-Qar where KD could be exchanged for between 2.5-10 Iraqi dinars during the occupation. After the allies launched the air war on 17 January 1991 the rate leapt to KD 1 = 20 Iraqi dinars.

The principal beneficiaries of the currency change were Iraqi troops. Officers and other ranks entered the co-operatives like animals and grabbed all the children's milk and baby items, together with cooking utensils and other food supplies,

leaving very little left for nationals. I asked one of them about this crazed shopping spree and he replied: "Where else can we find such great things -- Kuwait is a treasure trove which we have fallen into."

At 0800 on Friday 12 October 1990, the streets of Kuwait were congested with traffic to such an extent that a vehicle would take two hours to travel 500 metres in certain areas. My brother told me the reason. Special Forces troops at the checkpoints were seizing wallets from motorists and shredding all Kuwaiti Dinars. This appeared to be a retaliation for the decision by the exiled Kuwaiti Government to declare null and void all the currency held at the Central Bank of Kuwait which had been stolen by Saddam Hussein's army on the first day of the invasion. In other words the regime knew they could not use the stolen dinars outside Kuwait so it ordered as many as possible to be torn up in the streets. Nevertheless, at least one Iraqi soldier was spotted by Kuwaitis pocketing Kuwaiti Dinar notes that he was supposed to be shredding, proving the old adage, "once a thief, always a thief."

► *Petrol station restrictions*

The majority of Kuwaitis refused to change their car number plates to Iraqi registrations, despite abuse and interrogation by plainclothes police and Special Forces. I was among the Kuwaitis who refused to switch licence plates, because obeying such an Iraqi order would have brought shame on my head. The occupation forces kept extending the deadline each month for the changeover until issuing a final deadline of 22 January 1991. It was part and parcel of the Iraqi campaign to erase Kuwait's independent identity.

When they realised that only a few citizens were prepared to comply the Iraqis claimed the extension had been granted, because of congestion in the traffic department. Saddam Hussain's occupation forces then issued an order prohibiting supply of petrol to vehicles with Kuwaiti plates, with effect from Sunday 2 December 1990. Garages were barred from repairing or changing the oil of Kuwaiti-registered cars or trucks.

The Iraqi militia took up positions at the entrances to all petrol stations to enforce the decree. The ban was imposed strictly on the first two days but many Kuwaiti nationals managed to get fuel by bribing Iraqi militiamen, who barely received basic daily rations, with cigarettes, sugar and tea. The occupation authorities were forced to augment the militia with C.I.D. goons.

Quality petrol of 98 octane was totally sold out in Kuwait after the first month of the occupation. Only 90 octane petrol was on sale. The price rose from 40 to 90 fils a litre but the Iraqis evaded this by issuing stolen Kuwait National Petroleum Company staff coupons to their staff.

Those Kuwaitis who complied with the licence plate instructions often did so because of family circumstances, the need to drive or out of fear of reprisals. Those who did "legitimise" their transport played a major role in supplying food and essentials to others, especially after the allies launched the air attack on 17 January 1991. After that date no Kuwaiti vehicle was allowed on the streets.

▶ *Fabrication of charges against Kuwaitis*

Iraqi police tactics were arbitrary and unpredictable. Interrogation was aimed at extracting any confession or incriminating evidence that would lead the police to their goals. The most severe punishment was reserved for those who refused to co-operate. Two young Kuwaiti men from the military cadet corps who were not more than 19 years old were arrested on 13 November 1990 with a group of other youths. They were tortured in a number of ways, the least severe of which was a flogging and having cigarettes stubbed out on their bodies. They were then deported to Iraqi prisons where they suffered hunger, fear, thirst and more physical abuse for more than four months. The only reason for this treatment was the refusal by the two cadets to supply any information about other military personnel known to them.

A number of accusations were fabricated against them, such as joining in political opposition, taking part in the resistance and bearing arms. I saw one of them two days after his arrest. Signs of torture were obvious all over his emaciated body. I wept. It was the first time in my life that I had seen a brother being tortured in Kuwait and yet I was powerless to help him.

At 0800 on Monday 31 December 1990 in the Ardiya area residents were shocked at a particularly vicious murder. A Kuwaiti youth, not more than 19 years old, was executed by two shots in the head on the pavement outside his home, after being held for more than 30 days. Jassim Mohammed Al-Dashti was arrested on suspicion of writing slogans on the walls and because an Iraqi officer had been found murdered in his home district. The Iraqis required a scapegoat and this was Jassim Al-Dashti's fate. I saw his body lying on the ground covered with a white cloth with a number of plain clothes police

The martyr Jassim M. Al-Dashti

standing by and pretending to mount an investigation. The Iraqis would not allow the body to be moved for five hours and then ironically insisted on taking it to Basra for an autopsy.

Trumped up charges were not only laid against young men but elderly people were also accused with false crimes. An Iraqi stooge fabricated a report in which he accused a Kuwaiti woman of more than 50 years in age of "terrorism" and inciting other women to demonstrate. Her son Mish'al Al-Saqubi gave me a copy of the indictment. Dated 16 August 1990 it was signed off by Rashid, the Commanding Officer of the Abdullah Al-Salem police station, and addressed to Kuwait Police Headquarters:

" *Subject: Arrest of Terrorists*
During routine patrol Car No 4609 - - A.H., Type Caprice, was stopped and two women were discovered inside. The first was named Maha Ali Saleh and the other was her mother Shaikha Abdul-Aziz. An Indian was at the wheel. A search revealed a collection of photographs of "the agents" Jaber and Saad and a Kuwaiti flag. On arrival at the station one of them abused us calling us "invaders" and was very excited declaring that they would not forswear their allegiance to Jaber.

"They were dispatched to the Directorate of Police in the Capital. After that we received an anonymous telephone call to the effect that this woman was the same one guilty of inciting young men and

Shaikha Abdul-Aziz Saleh and her daughter Maha - among the first Kuwaiti women interned during the occupation

women to riot and distributing newsletters in various areas of Kuwait."

The Iraqis deported mother and daughter and held them in an unknown location, without any thought as to their health, before releasing them in Basra. Before their release they were subjected to appalling physical abuse.

Dr Khalid Al-Wasmi, a former National Assemblyman, was arrested at dawn one day in September 1990 but managed to avoid torture, despite being accused of leading a resistance group. One of the Palestinians who acted honourably during the occupation was a long-time resident of Kuwait. He said: "I left Palestine in the late 1940s after the Israeli occupation and heard subsequently of Israeli massacres of Palestinians in the occupied lands but I

have never witnessed in my life anything like the holocaust which took place in Kuwait."

Much of the blame for the atrocities can be laid at the feet of Saddam Hussain's half-brother Sabawi Ibrahim, head of the C.I.D. and his deputy Talib who acted on the direct orders of the military Governor of Kuwait Ali Hassan Al-Majeed.

Following the liberation on 26 February 1991, Kuwaiti nationals were horrified to find at the end of Damascus Street in an open area of garbage and wrecked cars a young man's body. It had been thrown to the ground with most of the head detached, leaving behind only a small part of the lower jaw. The marks of torture were clear for all to see. His finger and toe nails had been ripped off. About 50 metres away in the same area another young

Plate 31A. External view of the main torture centre at Rabia during the occupation

Plate 32. Inside the torture centre

Plate 33. A tool used by Iraqi CID men to disfigure male and female genitals

أداة للجهاز التناسلي

Plate 34. This "electric hat" was used to deliver shocks to the brain

Plate 35. An electric drill used to make holes in bones

Plate 36. Carpentry tools used to smash limbs and fingers and remove finger and toenails

48

Plate 37. Different kinds of plastic and wooden truncheons used for beating suspects and a broken glass bottle inserted in the anus

Plate 38. Scientific radiation instrument used to damage the eyes

Plate 39. High frequency instrument   used to destroy hearing - heating equipment used to deliver burns to the hands

Plate 40. This instrument was used to produce a fatal electric shock

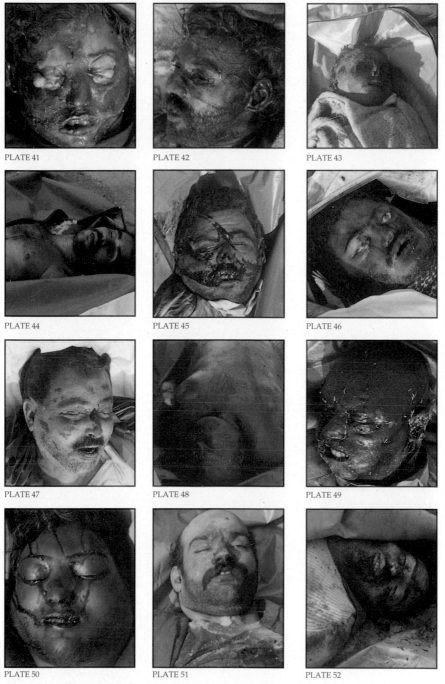

PLATE 41   PLATE 42   PLATE 43

PLATE 44   PLATE 45   PLATE 46

PLATE 47   PLATE 48   PLATE 49

PLATE 50   PLATE 51   PLATE 52

Plates 41-52. These pictures show examples of torture atrocities committed by Iraqi CID men

50

Plate 53. An Iraqi taxi attacked by resistance fighters in a residential suburb

Plate 54. The Salmiya District was changed to Al-Nasr Quarter as shown in this yellow plate

Plate 55. Al-Nida'a was the new name for Ahmadi

Plate 56. The Mubarak Al-Kabir Hospital's entrance - the name was changed to Al-Fida'a

man's body was thrown there with a bullet entry wound through the neck.

A volunteer working at the Mubarak Al-Kabir Hospital Jassim Al-Shatti said: "I was brought the body of a martyred woman Asrar Al-Qabandi with her head shattered by an axe. Her distinguishing features had been eliminated. She had been delivered the coup de grace with two bullets in the chest. She was accused of working with the resistance against the invaders."

Saddam Hussain's troops committed countless crimes in Kuwait.

A headless torso - the author saw it in Damascus Street, Surra, on 28 February 1991

Men and women were hung by the feet like animals in the Central Slaughterhouse. Concentrated sulphuric acid was poured over one Kuwaiti's body until it dissolved. Rape was committed against women and virgin girls. A seven months pregnant woman was tortured because her husband, a serving military man, was out of Kuwait. After abusing her they gang raped the woman until she aborted her fetus.

In the first week of December 1990 Iraqi troops began a concerted campaign of terror in Sabah Al-Salem, Bayan and Rumaithiya areas. They broke into homes of Kuwaitis and locked the master of the house in his lavatory while they stole all his possessions and raped the women. I know two teenage girls, aged between 15 and 17, who were bestially raped by Iraqi soldiers and left bleeding and screaming with shock and pain in the street. Their father had to leave Kuwait after his daughters were given medical treatment.

Assaults against women and virgin girls increased to such an extent that Mubarak Al-Kabir Hospital's maternity unit was closed. A Kuwaiti woman volunteer para-medic said: "Most of the rape cases we received were girls aged between 15 and 16."

The distinguished psychiatrist Dr Fowzia Al-Dura'ei told me she had personally interviewed at least five girls who had been brutally raped by Iraqis. A 21-year-old woman "gang raped" by 15 men was then abandoned in the Mishrif area.

Another, aged 19, a bride of only four months, was raped by 14 criminals at a flat in Hawalli.

A young Kuwaiti, 20 years old, was found with his face battered, forehead stove in, an eye ripped out and a broken nose. What could this young man have done? The Iraqis had even written his name across his stomach with razor blades. Can this be tolerated in a civilised world?

Fahd Al-Khamiri, an officer in the Interior Ministry, saw from the window of his prison cell at Al-Farwaniya Governorate in Al-Aardiy, a group of Iraqi soldiers filling up a hole in the ground with fire. After a few minutes they brought out a battered and beaten young Kuwaiti and threw him into the blaze. When he cried out in agony, an officer shot him through the head. This officer was identified as commander of Special Forces brigade Number 606.

Midad Yousef supplied three French expatriates with food and shelter from the Iraqi CID

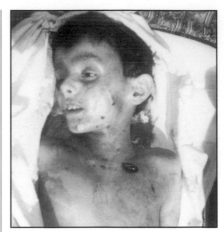

A seven-year-old Kuwaiti tortured with cigarette burns on his body and bullets through his chest - his "crime" was to write anti-Saddam graffiti on the walls

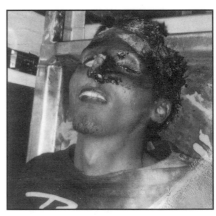

A young Kuwaiti resistance fighter with clear signs of torture on his nose, eyes and forehead

A colleague of mine Midad Yousef Khalid, an engineer at a Kuwait Air Force air base, spent 40 days in detention from 3 November 1990. He told me his story.

"Like many Kuwaiti men during the occupation, I volunteered to work as a manager for one of the co-operative societies. During the first three months, things went normally until one day a Lieutenant Hamid from the C.I.D. summoned me to attend a meeting at police headquarters. I did not suspect anything at first. The lieutenant and two others escorted me in my car until we reached the Governorate of the Capital. At that point I felt trapped. I entered an interview room and Hamid began screaming charges at me -- forging a driving licence, helping the resistance, not surrendering as a military man, hiding a member of the royal family and supplying him with food. I was also accused of discriminating against others in favour of Kuwaitis, handing out money to nationals and refusing to co-operate with the Iraqi authorities.

"I was blindfolded and shifted from one place to another during my detention. I was held for four days at the governorate building, then moved to the palace of the late Shaikh Mubarak Abdullah Al-Jaber at Mishrif for a single day. After that I was moved to the main torture centre in Kuwait, the Public Authority for Agriculture & Fisheries in the Rabiah area off the Fifth Ring Road. This centre was run by the Iraqi C.I.D. under a man called "Talib" who was nicknamed "Abu Mushtaq". I stayed there for 20 days and managed to memorise the telephone number -- 4741817. After that I was transferred to Jiwan Camp, back to Rabia and then to the Youth Prison at Sulaibiya between the Fifth and Sixth Ring Roads.

"I was interrogated seven times during my detention. They sought information about the names of officers I knew, the shaikh's palace I dealt with and other military secrets. When they extracted nothing from me, they offered me 2,000 Iraqi dinars a month to work for them and 50,000 Iraqi dinars for information about the shaikh's whereabouts. I was threatened with execution and they used psychological torture, threatening to deprive me of water unless I told them what they wanted to know. I remained silent and endured the torture without giving anything away."

I asked Midad about the torture methods used on him. He said: "When the Iraqi C.I.D. were crazed with drink, usually at dawn, they relished torturing people. At first the punishment was light. I was hit over the fingers with an electric cable about 200 times. I was made to count the blows. Next they used a stick. It was excruciatingly painful and afterwards red bubbles broke through my skin. Then they used an electric gun and pointed it at the nape of my neck, my knees and just over the kidney. That really hurt. Finally a pair of pliers was used to extract a toe nail."

Midad added: "God was by my side. After one month inside I was permitted to speak to my wife on the telephone. Others suffered far more than me in that place. I saw an Iranian hanging from a fan which was being rotated at speed. His offence -- to ask an Iraqi soldier which unit he came from. I also saw them beating a group of youths over the back and flogging an elderly man of more than 65 because he had been distributing cash. I also saw an Egyptian completely naked. He was in agony after the Iraqis had inserted a plastic hose into his anus. His offence -- carrying a pass to Al-Rehab Complex! The most appalling incident was to hear a 17-year-old virgin screaming as the Iraqi criminals ripped her vagina with a plastic garden hose, because she had written anti-Iraqi slogans on the wall."

There are thousands of such stories known to nationals who remained in Kuwait during the occupation but one that stands out is that of Captain Ahmed Qabazard whose home in Jaberiyah was put to the torch. The Iraqis gouged out one of his eyes, hacked off his penis and shot him through the head after accusing him of being a member of the resistance. Adel Al-Raqm was another Kuwaiti martyr who bled for 10 days before dying of wounds inflicted on him with an electric saw.

A Kuwaiti woman Mrs Makkiya Abdul Riza Al-Meil was arrested at her home in Sabah Al-Salem neighbourhood on 20 October 1990, accused of supplying the resistance with arms and ammunition, treating the wounded and forging I.D.s. She was subjected to vicious torture at the Rabiah main torture centre. This included pistol whipping, torture with a stick and steel band and a beating followed by having petrol poured over her body. The Iraqis also threatened to torture her children in front of her eyes.

Mrs Al-Meil was working with the 25 February Group including

Mrs Makkiya Al-Meil - severely tortured in Rabia

Khalid Abdul Hamid Al-Hajji, son of the director of Kuwait's Traffic Department. During her detention she saw both the Governor of Kuwait Ali Hassan Al-Majeed and the C.I.D. chief Sab'awi Ibrahim supervising torture at Rabiah. Mrs Al-Meil witnessed a group of blindfolded Kuwaiti girls being stripped naked and assaulted. She also saw detained men being padlocked to gas cylinders in the corridors. It took a huge bribe to Talib Abu Mushtaq -- Sab'awi's deputy -- to gain her freedom.

ERASING A NATION'S IDENTITY

The Kuwaiti citizen was not the only target of the Baghdad government. His homeland was the other. In order to erase Kuwait from the map, the Baathist regime determined on a plan to destroy and erase all the features and landmarks that characterised the State of Kuwait. It was a campaign against Kuwait that escalated as soon as it became clear that Kuwaitis remained loyal to their leaders.

Saddam Hussain's bureaucrats dispatched many Iraqi families as settlers to live in Kuwaiti residential suburbs, such as Al-Jahra, Sulaibikhat and Qurain but the Kuwaiti resistance terrified these families of colonists who believed their lives were in danger. Many decided to flee home rather than remain in Kuwait.

The Iraqis used other means to depopulate the country. Kuwaitis

The Mubarak Al-Kabir Hospital entrance with its name changed to Al-Fida'a Hospital

were allowed through the Nuwaiseeb border check point with Saudi Arabia but only after they had traversed rough desert roads. The occupation forces infiltrated a number of secret agents with forged Kuwaiti passports to observe the situation in the kingdom. The Saudi authorities foiled this plot by arresting them, acting on information supplied by Kuwaiti security men.

The Iraqis worked out a scheme to rob the homes of departing nationals by ordering them to surrender their civil I.D. cards before leaving. These showed their place of abode. Some nationals were even asked to assign all their property in Kuwait to the Iraqis, before getting permission to leave. When they left Kuwait, nationals were often denied access to their vehicles, passports, birth certificates and I.D., so as to cause maximum confusion to the reception centres in Saudi Arabia. This harassment continued from the first week of September 1990 until early January 1991 when the Kuwait-Saudi border closed.

▶ *Changes in bureaucracy*

On the "official merger" between Kuwait and Iraq on Tuesday 28 August 1990, the new governorate of Kuwait was segmented into three districts -- Kazimah (Kuwait City), Jahra and Al-Nida'a. A number of deputies was attached to each, as is the case in each of the Iraqi governorates.

The Iraqis changed the names of many residential suburbs, streets, schools and hospitals. The new names reflected the hatred of the Baghdad government for Kuwait's ruling family, since every school or other institution bearing the Al-Sabah name was altered.

The Iraqis introduced the term "quarter". Salmiya became Al-Nasr Quarter and among the other changes were Al-Khansa Quarter instead of Salwa, Al-Jumhouriya Quarter instead of Khaldiya, Al-Rasheed Quarter instead of Shuwaikh, Ahrar Quarter instead of Jaberiya, Al-Nida Township instead of Ahmadi and Al-Thawrah Quarter instead of Sabah Al-Salem neighbourhood.

It was with a considerable irony that Abdullah Al-Salem, one of Kuwait City's most exclusive residential suburbs, had its name changed to Basra Quarter, as if the Iraqis wanted to equate a well designed and laid out area of Kuwait to the dust and dirt of present-day Basra. The street names were also altered. When changing the names the Iraqi authorities replaced the original signs with different coloured plates and wrote the lettering in variegated characters to the original.

Salem Al-Mubarak was altered to 17 July Street, Hamad Al-Mubarak into Saqr Quraish Street, Faisal Bin Abdul Aziz Street into Babil Street and Nasir Al-Mubarak into Taimeem Street and so on.

The names of Kuwait's hospitals were given new titles. Mubarak Al-Kabir Hospital became Al-Fida'a General Hospital, the Addan was changed to Al-Nasr Hospital, the Al-Sabah turned into Saddam Hos-

A mosque with a new nameplate - it was formerly the Shaikha Badriya Al-Ahmed Al-Sabah Mosque

pital, while elsewhere in the city (Port) Abdullah became Saddam Port and Shuwaikh port became Al-Rashid Port!

The stupidity of the Iraqi regime even extended to altering the names of certain mosques. The Grand State Mosque was renamed Saddam Grand Mosque.

Despite these cosmetic alterations, the Iraqi forces themselves continued to use the old names when seeking directions. The new number plates which were eventually issued at either the Traffic Department in Shuwaikh or the Technical Section at Al-Jaberiya appeared to be of Kuwaiti manufacture but were of poor quality workmanship.

▶ *Forced changes of identity*

Kuwaiti citizens were instructed by the Iraqis to report to the Directorate of Nationality and Passports at Farwaniya to exchange their Kuwaiti I.D. for Iraqi nationality. A deadline of 23 November 1990 was set for

Example of an Iraqi vehicle number plate used during the occupation

changing their nationality or Kuwaitis would be considered aliens in their homeland. No true Kuwaiti exchanged his or her I.D.. Some left Kuwait because of the psychological pressure to rebel against this edict. The Iraqis punished those who failed to conform by denying them rations of food. Other nationalities were instructed to report to the "Arab Affairs Section" at the Kazima Sports Club to hand in their residence permits and exchange them for Iraqi documents.

An Egyptian expatriate told me: "I was compelled to go to Kazima Sports Club immediately after the morning prayer in order to complete the formalities, due to the long queues and prevalence of bribes. The Iraqis would humiliate certain Arab nationals, either by swearing at them or by throwing their passports down in a provocative way. After reporting for several days without making progress I was forced to pay 300 Iraqi dinars to a soldier, so as to sort out my documentation." Many residents, both Arab and expatriate, were harassed or arrested, because they refused to comply with these regulations.

▶ *Closure of foreign embassies*

In a desperate attempt to undermine Kuwait's sovereignty, Saddam Hussain's government ordered all foreign embassies in Kuwait to close within four days, with effect from 20 August 1990. Four days later the Iraqis threw a cordon round nine foreign embassies, including the American and the British. A total of 25 foreign embassies refused to close

Kazima Sports Club in Adailiyah - an Iraqi torture centre

Plate 57. Damage to the upper floors of the main Kuwait Airways building in the downtown

Plate 58. Damage at the entrance to Terminal One at Kuwait International Airport

Plate 59. The C.I.D. building at Salwa - burned three times by Kuwaiti resistance fighters to destroy secret documents

Plate 60. The Bayan Palace viewed from the 5th Ring Road with the damage visible to the observation gates

Plate 61. Offices wrecked and looted

Plate 62. Wreckage at a kindergarten in Kuwait

Plate 63. The College of Health Sciences was damaged during the first day of the invasion, later to become the Iraqi military headquarters

Plate 64. Damage at the Saudia airline building

Plate 65. Wreckage at the Souq Al-Wataniya in Kuwait City

Plate 66. Private homes were also hit

Plate 67. A palace belonging to the ruling Al-Sabah family was burned

Plate 68. A private residence

Plate 69. Damage to the outer wall of a private home

Plate 70. A private car showroom was burned   63

Plate 71. Another wrecked car showroom

Plate 72. Trenches on the beach near the Al-Salam Palace

Plate 73. Barbed wire used in beach defences

Plate 74. An observation post in Gulf Street

Plate 75. Al Danah restaurant - victim of arson

Plate 76. A damaged entertainment shop at Salmiya

Plate 77. A traditional sea-faring Kuwaiti village has been destroyed

Plate 78. The Kuwaiti Fishermen's Union was wrecked

Plate 79. Salmiya's traditional cafe - destroyed

Plate 80. The ancient Al-Maqsab Gate dating to the 1920s was demolished

Plate 81. The first American Hospital in Kuwait built pre-1920 was used as a base for the Iraqi militia

Plate 82. The burned out old souq in Kuwait City

Plate 83. The damaged entrance to Al-Gharabally Souq

Plate 84. Part of the damaged old souq

their consulates. The Iraqis retaliated with a number of aggressive actions against accredited diplomats to force them to relocate to Baghdad. The U.N. Security Council, meanwhile, issued Resolution 667 condemning these actions.

▶ *Vandalism on a grand scale*

The Iraqi forces singled out prominent landmarks in Kuwait for destruction, motivated by hatred for everything Kuwaiti. Many important buildings were vandalised or burned, such as the Kuwait Airways Corporation downtown office, car showrooms and ministry buildings. They dug trenches along the coastline and ruined green areas. Pavements and roads were destroyed as well as street furniture. Monuments or memorials dedicated to events in Kuwait's heritage were singled out for demolition. Even historic documents relating to Kuwait's proud independent history were vandalised. If the Guinness Book of Records regards the looting of the Nazi Reichsbank in April/May 1945 as the biggest robbery in history, there is now another contender, since on 2 August 1990 the Iraqis attempted to steal the assets of an entire country.

Crimes are often committed on the spur of the moment but in Kuwait's case a systematic transportation exercise which began on 2 August 1990 continued for more than 160 days. The mass movement of Kuwaiti property into Iraq only stopped two days before the air war was launched by the allies on 17

A truck used to transport stolen goods to Iraq

January 1991. Trucks with Jordanian numberplates would arrive in Kuwait with foodstuffs and leave full of stolen booty.

A Jordanian truck driver told me that the Iraqi authorities paid him 500 Iraqi Dinars a journey to take stolen goods from Kuwait to Baghdad or other governorates. In turn the lorry drivers sub-contracted five to seven men as stevedores to load their swag. These men who acted as willing accessories to theft were often nationals of an African Arab country, whose government sided with the Iraqis over the occupation of Kuwait. Needless to say, most of these robberies took place in broad daylight under the noses of the Iraqi militia or Special Forces. Only nationals who remained in the country were generally speaking immune from the attention of these criminals.

Among the first targets for the Iraqi invaders were the vaults at the Central Bank of Kuwait where the occupation forces seized KD 350 million in currency and KD 950 million in gold bullion, as well as a quantity of commemorative medals. More systematic crime followed:

● *Theft of 15 aircraft belonging to the Kuwait Airways Corporation which had been parked at Kuwait International Airport at the time of the invasion. All spare parts were taken from KAC's stores and the airport's navigation and control systems were wrecked.*

● *The contents of the Kuwait National Museum, the Islamic art collection, the scientific exhibits and the archaeological treasures on Failaka Island, many dating to the time of Alexander the Great, were stolen.*

● *Removal of the equipment and instruments from general and specialised hospitals. Theft of recordings and library tapes from Kuwait Radio and Television and nearly all equipment and cameras.*

● *Theft of foodstuffs from shops and supermarkets to feed Saddam Hussain's land forces in Kuwait. Nationals were forced to use only the co-operatives and were barred from buying from food stores in Shuwaikh and Sabhan. Special Forces personnel would confiscate any large quantities of food they saw being loaded into Kuwaiti cars.*

● *Looting of private shops and shopping malls throughout Kuwait and arson at many of them, especially the Gold market and the National Complex in the Capital, with special attention being paid to car, furniture and electrical showrooms.*

● *The seizure of public and private printing presses with all their inventories, machinery and accessories. Five printing presses survived. The Al-Qabas plant at Shuwaikh was used to print Al-Nida, the Iraqi newspaper in Kuwait, but in early 1991 the press was dismantled and stolen.*

The Iraqis issued forms to be filled in by nationals giving the identity of all members of their family, supposedly for food distribution. In reality these were used to

Four Iraqi special forces soldiers at rest near a Kuwaiti home but ready to kill at any time

target private properties for wholesale burglary. Some Kuwaitis left their unguarded homes with internal or external lights on to suggest occupancy but Iraqi C.I.D. men abused their authority to pinpoint as many empty homes as possible for the looting squads. A friend living in Rawdah told me of a visit by an Iraqi militia advising him not to obstruct Al-Amana (Honesty) truck that would visit a neighbouring property the next day. When the "honesty lorry" arrived it was used to empty the contents of a home whose owner had fled into exile.

Saddam Hussain's cynicism in calling trucks used for theft "honesty" vehicles was consistent with the behaviour of a man who appointed his brother Barazan Al-Takriti, former head of Iraqi Intelligence, to Human Rights Committees when his hands were still stained with the blood of his innocent victims.

The pillage in Kuwait extended to the economy as a whole. Spare parts, equipment and instrumentation was taken from Kuwait's oil refineries. A colleague who worked with the Kuwait National Petroleum Company Mohammed Al-Awadi saw 15 Iraqi trucks taking away spare parts from just one of the refineries. Dr Rashid Al-Ameeri, a former Minister of Oil, remarked grimly at a press briefing during the occupation that the only thing left for the Iraqis to take was the three Kuwait Water Towers.

In order to mislead the populace about their supposed zeal in suppressing crime the Iraqis executed a Lieutenant-Colonel Kazim, hanging him from a contractor's jib as a makeshift gallows in full view of the public at the Capital Governorate building. Kazim was branded a thief but his real crime had been to disobey orders from his superiors. A live video was also made of executions of alleged thieves by Special Forces personnel in Sabah Al-Salem and Salwa areas. Saddam Hussain's favourite viewing included such videos.

Damage at Shuwaikh Port in Kuwait

HARSH REALITIES OF OCCUPATION

The Iraqi invasion forces exerted control not only over all state functions and public life but also introduced many of their own corrupt practices, including the peddling of alcohol and soliciting and pimping of prostitutes.

Those Arab states which supported Iraq over the invasion of Kuwait may have been as unaware as many Kuwaitis of the extent of moral turpitude in Iraq. Kuwaitis soon became only too familiar with Iraqi corruption.

Drunkenness was common at Iraqi military checkpoints. When the soldiers were in their cups not only were they dangerous but they would curse Saddam Hussain and the Kuwait invasion plan. C.I.D. officers often only screwed up the courage to torture people by getting drunk first.

Alcoholic liquor which is banned in Kuwait but not in Iraq was soon on sale in shops, groceries and even at pavement stalls. Empty beers cans and bottles of spirits were soon found littering the sidewalks.

During the first months of the

Garbage thrown about at Entertainment City by Iraqi troops - typical of their undisciplined behaviour

72

occupation I noticed many strange women's faces, especially in the co-operative societies and the shops of Salem Al-Mubarak Street in Salmiya. Their behaviour was gauche, their clothes suggestive and they flirted openly with Iraqi soldiers, making lewd movements with their bodies. I heard much later that the Iraqi regime had actually sanctioned the import of these prostitutes, regardless of the risk of spreading sexually contagious diseases, and pandering to the sexual whims of Iraqi officers. A party of whores dressed in skimpy nightgowns was seen leaving an Islamic Society building in Rawdah accompanied by Iraqi officers.

The pick-up point for prostitutes was the Orthology Hospital Roundabout where these brazen tarts would park their cars by the roadside, talking loudly and offering their bodies for sale in broad daylight.

The disregard for Islamic tenets shown by Saddam Hussain's thugs did not stop at alcohol and whores but his troops even stopped Kuwaitis from going to the mosque, especially at dawn and dusk, owing to the curfew. The C.I.D. mounted street surveillance of worshippers. At Friday noon prayers most sermons steered clear of any mention of the occupation. The occupation authorities forced the preachers to refer to Jihad (Holy War) and praise The Leader (Saddam). Many mosque staff fled or hid to avoid going to the mosque to repeat such lies.

At one Friday prayers the Iraqi army scandalised the feelings of be-

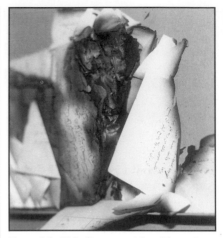

Parts of the Holy Quran were found burned at the Rabia Torture Centre

lievers by marching into Al-Mailam Mosque in Edailiyah wearing their filthy boots so they could photograph worshippers leaving the building.

Further sacrileges were carried out by the Iraqis who even assaulted the dead by demolishing a number of tombs belonging to members of the Al-Sabah family in Sulaibikhat Cemetery. Parts of the Holy Quran were found burned in the main torture centre at Rabia.

▶ *Pavement economy*

After the refusal of many merchants to open their shops, a new style of pavement stall started operating in many parts of Kuwait, selling almost every commodity required for home consumption. Among the largest were those behind the Passport office in Hawalli, at the Orthology Hospital Roundabout and opposite the Mishrif Exchange at Bayan. The Iraqis intended to move them to the Exhibition Fairgrounds at Mishrif but the U.N. deadline was approaching and the stalls completely disappeared from Tuesday 15 January 1991 returning in some areas after 27 January 1991 when it was clear that the air war would last for some time.

Prices were often three times as much as the co-operatives. The salesmen would buy in bulk from the co-ops for resale to the public.

The Iraqi vendors who sold eggs, chickens, dates and fruit would sit in the middle of rotting filth and garbage, as if it wasn't there. Most of them were from the southern Iraqi governorates. The filth at the Vegetable Market was indescribable. Flies covered every product -- to such an extent that it was difficult to tell one vegetable from another. Some of these insects had never been seen before in Kuwait and remained a plague until killed off by the winter weather in December 1990. Flies are usually prevalent in Kuwait in September -- the season which is called "sfiri" -- but during the occupation the "sfiri" continued for five months.

Disease also spread during the occupation because of uncollected household garbage. The Iraqi troops stole all the cleansing department's equipment and vehicles. Unless residents took their own rubbish to open spaces and burned it there was no other way of disposal. In this way Saddam Hussain turned the clock back thirty years, since that was how waste was removed in the early 1960s before Kuwait Municipality organ-ised a modern refuse collection service. When the Iraqis finally managed to organise a rubbish collection service of sorts, using trucks with Ministry of Local Government written on the side, it was not surprising to hear that they were simply dumping the junk on a runway at Kuwait International Airport instead of using the designated disposal sites.

▶ *Disrepect of traffic regulations*

In spite of the fact that the Iraqi police took possession of all traffic and emergency cars in Kuwait, the Iraqi policemen and Iraqi troops were an example of disrespect in their ignorance of the red traffic lights and driving against traffic and at mad speeds.

I once saw a collision between a stolen Iraqi patrol car and a car of a Kuwaiti woman. The result of which was the windshield of the car belonging to the lady was broken as well as other damage in the front. The main cause of this accident was high speed. When the lady came out of her car, she shouted in the face of the Iraqi officer and he returned by cursing her and warning her not to say any more.

Regretfully, some nationals and residents got used, during the Iraqi occupation, to ignoring traffic rules, as was done by the soldiers and policemen of the tyrant.

▶ *Distrust between communities*

Baghdad Television occasionally showed film of life in Kuwait during the occupation. A troupe of Palestin-

74

ian girls from Tolaitila (Toledo) Secondary School in Hawalli was shown dancing and singing the praises of Saddam Hussain. A few days later a rumour went round that eight women students from the Toledo School had been killed in a revenge attack by the resistance.

This turned out to be a story put round by the Iraqi C.I.D. to sow the seeds of distrust between Kuwaitis and Palestinians. Assassination of school girls was not a resistance activity and it is difficult to believe how it could have been done with checkpoints surrounding the school in question. The killings were almost certainly the work of the Iraqi C.I.D..

Demonstrations became a way of life in Kuwait. When the U.N. Security Council passed Resolution 678

UN Security Council meeting which gave an ultimatum to Iraq to quit Kuwait by 15 January 1991

sanctioning force against Iraq, the Iraqis stage managed a protest in Kuwait. On 30 November 1990 Special Forces troops rounded up dozens of nationals and made them take part in an anti George Bush demo at gunpoint.

▶ *Bribery and blackmail*

Kuwaitis often had to pay blackmail amounting to hundreds of thou-sands of Iraqi dinars to free their children from detention. Officers usually designated to whom the money should be paid. Some of them preferred payment in kind rather than cash -- video recorders or televisions being a favourite alternative. Kuwaitis also bartered their vehicles to get relatives out of jail. Mahmoud Qabazard, whose son Ahmed died a martyr's death, was arrested with his sons on 10 October 1990 and only got out of Rumaithiya Police Station on payment of 80,000 Iraqi dinars. One of the reasons for this avarice by the Iraqis was the low pay given to the ordinary Iraqi officer and other ranks compared to the Republican Guard and the C.I.D..

▶ *Food rationing*

A sudden food shortage occurred because the Iraqis had allowed the army to raid central stores. A directive was issued by the Iraqi Ministry of Commerce and the so called Association of Consumer Societies laying down the type and quantity of food to be handed out to each individual. A personal monthly quota was 75 grammes of tea, 750 grammes of sugar and a single bar of soap. Kuwaitis failed to take advantage of this offer as to obtain such rations would involve obtaining an Iraqi I.D. card.

▶ *Curfews*

From the first day of the occupation until 17 November 1990 a daily curfew was imposed on Kuwait lasting from 11 p.m. to 6 a.m.. To enforce this regime checkpoints were estab-

Plate 85. The Orthology Roundabout where the Iraqis launched their attack on Jiwan Camp - later it was a pick-up point for Iraqi hookers

Plate 86. Dirt everywhere - a common sight in occupied Kuwait

Plate 87. The Cabinet Building with Saddam Hussain's portrait

Plate 88. Saddam's image again at the old Ministry of Information building in Al-Sharq

Plate 89. Saddam's portrait near the Orthology Roundabout

Plate 90. Crowds at a petrol station during the occupation

Plate 91. Damage to the parking area at Kuwait International Airport

Plate 92. The Al-Qabas press building where Al-Nida'a was produced - at the left of the building is the place where the printing machines were stolen before the allied air attack started

Plate 93. The Ministry of Information studio complex where the "Mother of Battles" statement was broadcast

An issue of Al Nida'a newspaper

lished in all streets. Wooden barricades and metal drums stolen from the Kuwait Traffic Department were placed on flyovers to hinder the free movement of vehicles. With the increase in sniping the control system was rationalised and improved. Special Forces personnel were in charge of the checkpoints, searching for weapons, ammunition and newsletters, as well as checking motorists' I.D. and paperwork. From 15-28 December all checkpoints were withdrawn but this was a ruse by the C.I.D for on 29 December 1990 surveillance was restored.

The removal of the checkpoints had encouraged a large number of Kuwaiti military men, including army officers, to return home but sadly they were subsequently rounded up in a massive C.I.D. raid. Among the captives was Lieutenant-Colonel Abdul Mohsin Al-Mosab'ehi, an officer in Kuwait Army Intelligence.

In the first months of the occupation there was a difference in summer time, with Baghdad one hour ahead of Kuwait. I was stopped by an Iraqi officer who said: "What do you think the time is? Don't you know there is a curfew at 11 p.m.?" I replied: "It is 10.30 p.m. now." He said: "The time according to Baghdad is 11.30 p.m.!"

▶ *Saddam's portrait -- everywhere*

Portraits of Saddam Hussain, a common sight in Iraq, were soon found everywhere. They were sited at hospitals, co-operatives, schools, public squares and at ministry buildings but soon guards were required to ensure their safety.

The inscriptions often said they were a gift from a governorate to the people of Kuwait, as was the case at the old Ministry of Information building in Sharq, at the entrance to the Mubarak Al-Kabir Hospital, near the outer wall of the Ministries Complex opposite the Governorate of the Capital, at the Orthology Hospital Roundabout and by the Salmiya Cinema.

Some of these portraits were smashed or defaced by resistance men but the occupying forces threatened death to anyone tampering with either the pictures or the numerous Iraqi flags hoisted over public buildings.

▶ *Airport operations*

Flights to and from Baghdad were operated from Kuwait International Airport during the early months of the occupation. In October 1990, the Iraqi authorities were forced close the airport and divert civil flights to the Ali Al-Salem Airbase.

During the time the airport was operating passengers had to walk one kilometre to the terminal with their baggage and pay the air fare ticket of 40 Iraqi dinars before embarking.

Passenger traffic from Baghdad was busy after the third week of the invasion. Iraqi merchants arrived to bid at auctions held in the Holiday Inn Hotel. A friend who attended an auction told how the assets of a Kuwaiti company importing airconditioners were knocked down for 1

Everyday scene during the occupation - bread queues at a bakery

million Iraqi Dinars, whereas the company's actual paid-up capital was KD 5 million. Travellers who went by air to Baghdad found it hard to get back, since seats were block booked by Iraqi civil servants and soldiers.

▶ Congestion and queues

Queuing became a national pastime for Kuwaitis. Panic at the thought of Iraqi orders closing bakeries, co-operatives or petrol stations led to hoarding. Heads of families often got their whole clan in line. I once spent 90 minutes queuing at a bakery only to find the ration cut from 10 loaves to three.

Kuwaitis were denied access to bakeries after 14 January 1991 when the Iraqis dismantled and stole the machinery from the Kuwait Flour Mills at Shuwaikh. After that date the company's remaining equipment worked exclusively for the Iraqi forces. Flour became a precious commodity and after the air war began on 17 January 1991 prices soared to 900 Iraqi dinars a sack.

I remembered in that bread queue an article in Al-Siyassah newspaper by the distinguished Kuwaiti journalist and MP Mohammed Al-Berjis who described how H.H. The Amir once spotted five Kuwaitis in a bread queue. He was so horrified that he ordered the immediate opening of new outlets. As I recalled that act of generosity my eyes filled with tears and I said:" Bless you, Kuwait."

IRAQ'S TISSUE
OF LIES

The Iraqi forces only offered actual battle for a matter of days -- during the invasion on 2 August 1990 and after the allies launched the land battle. By contrast the media war waged by Iraq lasted more than 4,896 hours. The Baghdad regime mobilised all human and material resources in the propaganda war, exploiting television, radio and the press to mislead world opinion about the tragedy of Kuwait, as well as about domestic events in Iraq during the occupation. Saddam Hussain posed as the defender of Islam, a Muslim warrior confronting the infidel, a posture that appealed to many gullible people in Islamic countries in Asia and parts of the Arab world. Indeed some of the pro-Saddam demonstrations in Arab or Muslim states were in fact paid for in advance by Saddam's agents or diplomats.

Saddam Hussain's media corps staged a massive cover-up of the crimes which took place during the occupation. Journalists were subjected to severe restrictions and the Red Cross and Human Rights Committees were barred from the country on the grounds that it was a military exclusion zone. Kuwaitis smuggled video tapes out of the country showing clearly the extent of the damage which resulted in thorough searches of all Kuwaitis leaving the country. In response the Iraqi media highlighted the arrival of foreign forces in the Gulf seeking to prove the existence of an "Imperialist-Zionist conspiracy" against Baghdad. All fair minded people, however, appreciated the wisdom showed by King Fahd of Saudi Arabia in calling for help from Arab, Islamic and friendly powers. It was the Saudi monarch's duty as Custodian of the Two Holy Shrines to protect the cities of Makkah and Medina from the filth of Saddam Hussain's armies.

▶ *Attacking the oil states*

Saddam Hussain claimed that poverty in some Arab states was the result of an unequal distribution of oil wealth. The majority of Arab oil was controlled by a small group of countries controlled largely by "Amirs and oil shaikhs." The Iraqi leader purported to show that the occupation of Kuwait on 2 August 1990 was aimed at bringing about a more equitable distribution of wealth within the Arab nation.

Saddam Hussain, of course, ig-

King Fahd of Saudi Arabia, Custodian of the Two Holy Mosques -
his was the historic decision to invite the allied forces to the region

nored the huge subventions paid to his government by the Gulf states, most prominent of which were Saudi Arabia and Kuwait. What Saudi Arabia and Kuwait gave from their oil revenues, Iraq squandered on wars that destroyed the Iraqi economy and bankrupted its people. He also conveniently omitted to mention Iraq's great resources of water and manpower and that at one time oil itself earned Baghdad $28 billion a year.

Instead of using Iraq's wealth wisely for the benefit of his people or in aid to other Arab states Saddam Hussain had lavished millions on his family, relatives and Ba'ath Party cronies. He bribed terrorist organisations to do his dirty work by proxy, constructed palaces and amassed a huge arsenal not to protect Iraq and safeguard Arab interests but to wreak havoc instead.

▶ *Al-Nida'a is born*

In order to publicise Saddam's speeches and Ba'ath Party propaganda the newspaper Al-Nida'a was published in Kuwait. Its subsidiary tasks were to propagate circulars, lies and rumours, lower the morale of Kuwaitis and undermine their patriotism and loyalty to the ruling family. The newspaper was distributed free at co-operatives and checkpoints but most nationals spurned it at first. Later on, instead of burning or binning Al-Nida'a, Kuwaitis were forced to read it to find out what was going on in their own country.

Al-Nida'a was printed at Al-Qabas Newspaper Printing Press

with Hamed Al-Mulla, the Iraqi embassy in Kuwait's press adviser, playing a senior role in the newspaper's production until the end of December 1990. He was supported by a number of "agents" who were working at Al-Qabas and were well known for their disloyalty in Kuwait press circles. Many principled Kuwaiti and expatriate Arab journalists moved house and changed telephone numbers and some left the country rather than co-operate with Hamed Al-Mulla.

▶ *Radio transmissions*

The occupation regime established three radio stations to disseminate its propaganda to the outside world. The Voice of Al-Madina Al-Munawara, was aimed at Saudi Arabia; the English language Voice of Peace was directed at expatriates detained as human shields in Iraq, as well as the coalition forces. The Voice of Peace attempted to play on the emotions of allied personnel warning them that their children would become orphans due to the policies pursued by President Bush and Prime Minister Thatcher. The third was the Mother of Battles Station which began broadcasting after the air war started and was beamed at Iraqi forces from the main radio studios in Kuwait.

The Mother of Battles broadcast was relayed by loudspeaker to all schools used as barracks by Iraqi troops in Kuwait. Propaganda speeches and songs were its stock in trade.

The allies countered with Voice of Free Iraq transmitted 12 hours a day from Jeddah, Saudi Arabia, which shed light on the true situation in Iraq, the C.I.D.'s tactics against ordinary people and their brutal methods of suppression. The Kuwaiti broadcaster Salwa Hussain read the news on Voice of Free Iraq.

Kuwait Radio from Dammam was not well received due to Iraqi jamming but came through strongly a few days into the air war and from then until liberation on 26 February 1991. Kuwait Radio was the best source of information during the occupation, since the Iraqis were successful in stopping the circulation of information inside Kuwait. No newspapers or magazines existed and television reception from the neighbouring Gulf states was jammed most of the time. The One O'Clock News from Kuwait Radio as presented by Ali Hassan, Yousuf Mustafa, Nasser Al-Ajmi, Mohammed Al-Qahtani and Fatma Al-Qattan was something to look forward to with anticipation. Another highlight was reports from Kuwait Radio's overseas correspondents around the world, such as Saad Khalaf, Ibrahim Al-Mahmoodi, Talla'a Al-Diehani, Mahmood Al-Hamar, Ferial Al-Attar and others who supplied the latest developments in the liberation struggle.

Another boost to national morale during the initial period of the occupation came from the speeches of Shaikh Ahmed Al-Qattan. They were like a balm for our wounds. Many Kuwaitis also listened in to the news bulletins of the BBC Arabic Service, and the Voice of America. I tuned in regularly to Majid Sarhan from the BBC, together with his colleagues Hassan Mo'awad and Kasim Jaffer who reported faithfully on world reaction to the Iraqi attack on Kuwait.

Some radio stations had a negative effect on Kuwaiti morale by broadcasting news items that gave tip offs to the occupation forces and the police. A particular report centred on the arrival of a large number of Kuwaitis in Iran who had crossed the Iraqi border with false papers. As a result 2,400 Kuwaitis, among them women and children, were halted without water for more than 48 hours near the Iraq-Iran border as a reprisal. Thanks to providence they were spared further abuse and torture and allowed to return to Kuwait.

▶ *Television propaganda*

Baghdad Television made a great play on alleged Kuwaiti support for the annexation. It was clear, however, that interviews with prominent Kuwaitis had been done under duress. Apart from the former Kuwaiti ambassador to Iraq Ibrahim Al-Ba'hoo and Shaikh Salem Fahd Al-Salem Al-Sabah, former chairman of the Volleyball Federation, the Iraqis also interviewed a Kuwaiti national Salem Al-Dhafeeri who publicly attacked Kuwaiti government officials. Al-Dhafeeri had been sentenced to jail as a common criminal in Kuwait for fraud and obtaining Kuwaiti nationality by deception. The Iraqis released him after the invasion and I saw him in a black Mercedes 280 SEL with a driver and military escort.

Iraqi Television showed tape of Saddam Hussain's inspection tour of his forces on the Corniche at Salmiya on the morning of Tuesday 15 January 1991. I was saddened at the sight of "the tyrant" among his soldiers in Arabian Gulf Street near the Salmiya public cafe as if he was taunting Kuwaitis, saying: "Here I am on your land."

The Iraqis broadcast a programme called "Welcome, Brothers!" from Kuwait TV in which interviews were conducted with soldiers. It caused Kuwaitis much mirth. In an attempt to rebut international news reports that Iraqi soldiers were starved of rations, the programme showed soldiers standing round a tray of aubergine and rice. "What's for lunch today?", asked the Iraqi actor-presenter. "Chicken, thank God," was the reply. When asked where the aubergine had come from a soldier answered: "We planted it, right there," pointing to some arid land with no water. Kuwaitis did not need a degree in agriculture to know this was false. Aubergines were out of season. Some wryly wondered which farm the chicken had been stolen from?

▶ *Iraqi morale collapses*

The Iraqi army's morale in Kuwait sank despite the campaign of lies. Some soldiers knew the truth but were afraid for their families back home. Disillusion for many set in as early as 15 August when Saddam Hussain squared his account with

Iran -- since the Iraqi military had suffered countless dead in the futile 1980-88 Gulf war. Abdullah Al-Mohailan, a Kuwaiti official working in information, told how one of his friends met an Iraqi soldier at a checkpoint in Mishrif. The soldier demanded a cigarette and told the Kuwaiti:" Shout at me and say you are a donkey, son of a donkey!" When the nervous Kuwaiti was eventually persuaded to join in this pantomime the soldier replied: "Do you know why I am a donkey? I was a prisoner of war in Iran for eight years. When I returned to Iraq I found my wife had married another man so I went to the military recruiting office. They gave me this uniform, this weapon and sent me to Kuwait. Now I am standing in front of you. Am I not a donkey, son of a donkey?"

Iraqi troops became convinced they would all die given the might of the opposing forces. A friend working at Al-Addan Public Hospital treated an Iraqi soldier complaining of a kidney stone. He gave him the necessary medicine and advised him to drink plenty of water. The soldier laughed:" Where can I get water? We have been three months in the trenches and we receive very little water." After that he looked furtively to left and right and asked:" Tell me, when will Bush start the attack and deliver us from the misery we are suffering in the trenches?"

▶ *Playing to the gallery*

The Iraqi media hype surrounding

The Saudi ambassador to Bahrain Dr Ghazi Al-Gosaibi

Saddam Hussain was exposed by commentators such as Dr Ghazi Al-Gosaibi, the Saudi essayist, diplomat and former minister but as a strategy it was often successful. The Palestinian layman believed the case for linkage between the freedom of Kuwait and the liberation of Palestine. Fundamentalist Muslims were also taken in by Saddam Hussain, believing that he had returned to God, renewed his faith or to use a Christian term was "born again." When trying to understand how so many intelligent people were taken in by Iraqi propaganda it may be worth remembering the great poet Al-Mutanabbi who wrote: "An essay has a successful impact on the reader if it finds approval in his heart."

The seductive talent of Saddam was to appeal to those who had nothing to lose by supporting a man who promised them the earth. Dr Al-Gosaibi wrote: "The confrontation indeed became transformed into an actual mother of battles but it was a battle of a different kind. Anyone who had a battle with Israel metaphorically speaking entered Kuwait; anyone who fought his regime or western culture entered Kuwait. And so behind Saddam Hussain walked the Palestinians who wanted to return to Acre, and the North African who felt humiliated to work in the Port of Marseilles and the radical who dreamed of implementing sharia in Sudan and all those who felt hatred to anyone in the Gulf whether reasoned or not."

I take this opportunity to praise Dr Al-Gosaibi, the Saudi ambassador to Bahrain, for his courageous stand over the Iraqi occupation. He deployed his literary talents to our cause in a way that the people of Kuwait will never forget. God bless him!

SOLIDARITY IN FACE OF CRISIS

The Kuwaiti people set an outstanding example of co-operation and self sacrifice during the 208 day occupation. Few peoples in recent times have suffered terrorism, murder, execution and torture on such a scale. Yet for many Kuwaitis the crisis led to a discovery of hidden strengths and reservoirs of courage. Some realised for the first time the benefits of teamwork and self reliance. What follows is only a small insight into the unity and togetherness expressed in Kuwait's hour of need.

▶ *Steadfastness of Kuwaiti women*

Saddam Hussain claimed that the 500,000 Kuwaitis had 1 million servants between them. Although there was an element of truth in this criticism, as a result of the invasion thousands of Asian servants who were working in Kuwait left the country. Few of them remained for

Iraqi soldiers deploy in Kuwait in the early days of the occupation.

the duration of the occupation.

Life did not collapse without them. Kuwaiti women proved themselves first class housewives. They cooked, washed, baked bread, and supervised childcare to such an extent that most Kuwaiti households lived better than when they had servants. The Kuwaiti woman was transformed from her old self before "Black Thursday". She faced up to Saddam's thugs, challenging their injustice and failed to be intimated even when faced with the execution of her husband, detention of her sons or her brother's torture. Above all Kuwaiti women retained their pride and dignity in the face of provocation, assault and outrage.

Kuwait will always remember the sacrifice of women martyrs, such as Wafa Al-Amir, Asrar Al-Qabandi, Suad Al-Hassan and many others.

Wafa Ahmed Al-Amir, a 23-year-old X-Ray technician, was arrested at a home in Cordoba on 11 January 1991. She was buried at Riqqa cemetery on 6 February 1991 -- signs of torture were visible on her neck. Wafa took part in the guerrilla bomb attack on the Kuwait International Hotel in November 1990 which resulted in the assassination of a number of Iraqi officers and civilians. She also blasted two restaurants in the Kheitan and Hasawi areas. She offered safe houses for resistance fighters, worked as a weapons porter and forged I.D. cards.

Suad Ali Al-Hassan, a 19-year-old second year student at Kuwait University, was arrested on 10 January 1991. She was buried at Riqqa cemetery on 14 February 1991 after having been found at Keifan, murdered with a chain round her neck and torture marks on her face. She was accused of helping Wafa

The martyr Wafa A. Al-Amir

The martyr Al-Hassan

Ahmed Al-Amir to carry weapons for the resistance. Suad was arrested on the basis of a forged letter from her detained husband who had been captured on 2 August 1990. She and her mother were interrogated by a notorious Iraqi bully called Ziad, and afterwards by Lieutenant Haider Al-Tamimi.

Kuwait will never forget the young women who acted as couriers and weapons porters for the resistance. During the occupation such women proved they could take responsibility. Those who were caught by the Iraqis often paid for their patriotism with their lives. Others were abused and tortured. Many were raped. Such women were scarcely "the empty headed pleasure seekers" who only care for fashion and jewellry, the image depicted in some western and Arab newspapers.

Among the heroines of the occupation were Mrs Dalal Al-Zabin, widow of the late Kuwaiti literary figure Ahmed Al-Adwani. She turned her home into a first aid training centre, a risky undertaking since the Iraqis considered such "schools" subversive and an extension of the resistance. Another woman Zainab Hamed Aman took charge of the social welfare homes and outstanding work was done by her colleagues Fadila Bilal Al-Khamees, Sana'a Badr Al-Kharqawi, Haifa Gharib and Khalid Ali Mehdi.

I asked Zainab how she managed to keep the social welfare homes for children, the handicapped and mentally disabled as well as a reha-

Zainab Hamed Aman - she is dressed in a black skirt and white shirt in the centre of the picture

bilitation centre, going during the occupation. She said:" I thank God for giving us new life. I survived with my colleagues under trying conditions which we managed to endure despite threats of murder and the mental stress of dealing on a daily basis with the Iraqis. We were strengthened by continuous readings of the Holy Quran. The social welfare homes were the last to be entered by the Iraqis in the first week of September 1990 and they were the last to fly the Iraqi flags. God blinded them so they did not rob or take anything from our buildings, not even their contents which are worth millions of dinars. With help from volunteers we managed to conceal our valuable equipment and hide the 17-18-year old girls who were our boarders. Iraqi soldiers climbed over our walls more than once seeking our virgins but thank God they were unmolested.

"We tried through all means possible to avoid having any truck with the invaders -- civilian or military. I refused, as did all my colleagues, to accept any pay from them and remained in the residential homes taking care of our clients, including the elderly and physically disabled. We hardly returned to our own homes at all except for family emergencies.

"The Iraqis once tried to force me to pull down the portrait of H.H. The Amir as well as the Kuwaiti flag, but I refused and when they threatened to kill me I told them I wasn't afraid of death and so there was no need to threaten me.

"On one occasion they asked me to take part in a ceremony to unveil a portrait of the tyrant (Saddam Hussain) in front of our buildings but thank God it poured with rain that day and the formalities were cancelled.

"When the Iraqis asked us for a full list of boarders at the homes we provided false information to stop them stealing things and inundating us with residential cases from Iraq. We hit on one way of deterring official visitors. We started such tours in the section for severely retarded men. No sooner did the visitors spot the naked men than they made their excuses and left."

Zainab said the homes were used to shelter resistance fighters and military men wanted by the Iraqis. They were disguised as voluntary workers. She expressed her thanks to all citizens and other residents who helped with donations despite harassment from the C.I.D. who tailed people entering or leaving the complex.

▶ *Treating wounded heroes*

Some doctors began treating the sick and wounded in their homes during the occupation because of obstruction offered to them by the Iraqis in their hospitals or clinics. Immunisation of young children -- a programme in which Kuwait leads the Arab world -- was maintained in this way.

When the C.I.D. clamped down on the treatment of resistance fighters in hospital, Kuwaiti doctors did not sit idly by but did everything possible to bring succour to the injured. Another physician Dr Hisham Al-Obaidan paid for his self-sacrifice with his life.

Dr Waleed Mohammed Bishara told how they managed. He said: "We worked in complete confidence. We had to smuggle certain surgical equipment and medicines out of the hospital to treat the wounded, especially after the C.I.D. surveillance began in earnest. We also had to hoard supplies of atropine sulphate as an antidote to possible nerve gas attack. I kept in close contact with the resistance who told me about their casualties. I would ask for them to be brought to a certain place where they could be treated in secret and in safety."

Dr Bishara was questioned by the Iraqis at a checkpoint about the vaccine and needles he was carrying. His name and address was taken and a few days later his house was raided. Luckily Dr Bishara had already fled the city to join the Kuwaiti forces taking part in Operation Desert Storm.

▶ Civil disobedience

Kuwaitis refused to obey the Iraqi order to report normally for work. Only those services vitally required for the welfare of citizens were manned -- the medical profession and the Water and Electricity Department being two examples. By reporting for duty in horrendous conditions, the staff at the Ministry of Water & Electricity managed to reduce the damage and destruction carried out by the Iraqis. Among the stalwart nationals were Faisal Al-Mudaf, an engineer with the ministry, Engineer Mus'ab Al-Yaseen of the Kuwait Oil Company and Engineer Ahmed Ali Al-Selahi of the Salt and Chlorine Plant. The Kuwaiti Fire Brigade also did its best to extinguish blazes started by Iraqi arsonists.

▶ Learning new skills

In the first six weeks of the occupation the majority of the foreign workforce left the country, leaving Kuwait virtually at a standstill. Groceries were shut, together with bakeries, laundries, hairdressers, motor repair shops and garages. Kuwaiti men had to learn new skills and dirty their hands but many Kuwaiti men took to this with enthusiasm. By kindling a new team spirit Kuwaitis got down to work in bakeries and tackled many manual jobs

previously done by expatriates. It provided a good omen for the reconstruction work to come after liberation.

▶ Free petrol and food

Many Kuwaitis had insufficient money to buy food in the first weeks of the invasion. The co-operatives opened their doors to residents and expatriates alike, allowing them up to KD 10 credit a day to be re-paid after liberation. The co-operatives were a linch-pin for all Kuwaitis, helping the socially deprived, offering commodities at cost price and even bribing Iraqi officers to release detainees. The co-operatives were staffed by volunteers who temporarily abandoned their professions to work for the common good. Petrol stations also dispensed fuel free for the first few weeks until they were taken over by the Iraqis. Young Kuwaiti men served the community in the first few weeks of the occupation by acting as couriers for food supplies available from the co-operatives.

▶ Cash subsidies

The Kuwaiti government in exile managed to organise a cash distribution system for those left behind. A central committee comprising a number of individuals, including a member of the Al-Sabah family, took responsibility for handing out money in the residential suburbs. In each district there was a group of men responsible for delivering the cash, despite the risks attached to an activity punishable by a death sentence for "economic sabotage" if caught by the Iraqis.

Despite the secrecy and stealth applied to this operation many were arrested. Among the first sources of money to be used were the cash tills at petrol stations operated by the Kuwait National Petroleum Company. Iraqi soldiers were astounded that nationals were still able to purchase goods from the co-operatives. Their jealous barbs included remarks like," how do you get money, if you just sit at home and refuse to work?" Kuwaiti families received on average regular payments of between 400-700 Iraqi dinars. Some families missed out because they frequently moved house but every effort was made to follow up on needy individuals.

As soon as news came of a family with a member killed or arrested special assistance was on hand. Neighbours rallied round with meals or cooking equipment and provided them with cash and comfort. A number of Kuwaitis organised buses to transport families to visit their relatives taken prisoner and deported to Iraq. My mother, sister and brother travelled in this way to Al-Rasheed Detention Centre in Baghdad to see my other brother who was a prisoner. Morale there was high and Kuwaiti inmates were less worried about themselves than their families back in Kuwait, as they had heard of torture and human rights abuses in the occupied territory. Among those who helped Kuwaiti military men hide, as well as refugees from Failaka Island were staff at the General Authority of Housing.

▶ Prison visits

Prison visits were not possible until the beginning of October 1990, because of the information blackout imposed by the Iraqis. Fears for the safety of Kuwaitis seized in the early weeks of the invasion were growing by the day. Once visits were allowed a major role was played by Mahmoud Qabazard, whose son was killed in action. Despite his personal grief Qabazard helped Kuwaiti families to make the trip to Mosul to visit the 638 Kuwaiti officers held there, whose ranks ranged from lieutenant to colonel. Later these prisoners of war (POWs) were moved to the Ba'aqouba POW Camp near Baghdad.

Qabazard recalls:" One of my sons was an officer taken prisoner on 2

Mahmoud Qabazard - he helped arrange visits to Kuwaiti prisoners in Baghdad

August 1990. I did not know his whereabouts and sympathised with other parents who were equally concerned about their missing sons. I tried various means to facilitate visits to our captive sons. Eventually this was made possible by a senior Ba'ath Party official Abu Yasir who worked for Saddam Hussain for 14 year before retiring. He used his influence to shift the 638 Kuwaiti officers billeted at Mosul to Ba'aqouba. An office was opened in the Kazim area to register Kuwaiti families who wanted to visit their relatives.

" Abu Yasir laid down one condition for the visits: a thief's blackmail of 100,000 Iraqi dinars, four Chevrolet saloons and two Toyota pick-ups for his exclusive use. I fulfilled the agreement and paid this ransom the very next day."

Help of a different kind, with no strings attached, came from Riyadh Mohamed Sultan Al-Eisa, director of The Sultan Centre, Kuwait's best known supermarket and department store, who contacted families by phone and offered them hampers of food for the captives, free of charge. The Sultan Centre spent more than 1 million Iraqi dinars on aid for distressed Kuwaiti families some of it channelled through Shaikh Ali Al-Salem Al-Ali Al- Sabah. Al-Eisa was arrested by the Iraqis three times and accused of financing 'terrorist acts."

▶ *Help from companies*

The Kuwait Danish Dairy Company (KDDC) was one of the companies that broke the back of the black market in food by offering a basket of milk, yoghourt, laban and various fruit juices at bargain prices, not exceeding five Iraqi dinars. KDDC opened a direct outlet for its products at Shuwaikh. The prices compared very favourably with the pavement stalls and the souq where milk retailed at 3 dinars a litre.

The Iraqis eventually dismantled the KDDC's equipment at its factory in the Subhan Industrial Area and stole its equipment and raw materials. This fate was also meted out to 400 other factories in the same area. Other food companies, for example Americana, gave out free supplies of meat while the Kuwait Flour Mills distributed flour.

The executive director of KDDC Ezzat Mohamed Jaafar was arrested on 28 December 1990 together with his son Mohamed and accused of

Riyadh Mohamed Sultan Al-Eisa

Ezzat Mohamed Jaafar, special assistant to the former Amir of Kuwait HH Shaikh Ahmad Al-Jaber Al-Sabah

Historic photograph from 1938 (and from the collection of Yousef Shihab) with Iz'zat Jaffar seated in the centre with HH The Amir (left) and former Foreign Affairs Minister Shaikh Sabah Al-Ahmed (right).

communicating with HH the Amir, as well as handing out money to citizens and subidising the resistance. He was also accused of forging KDDC's legal documents to protect shares held by its co-owner Shaikh Nasser Sabah Al-Ahmed Al-Sabah.

Jaafar kept his product prices as low as possible during the occupation, selling a "family package" comprising a range of dairy goods sold for five Iraqi dinars only. When arrested and taken to the Abu Ghreeb jail in Baghdad, Jaafar staged a hunger strike. He would have fallen seriously ill had it not been for the help given to him by another arrested Kuwaiti Mohamed Al-Fajji.

Al-Fajji, born in 1953, was a leading Kuwaiti merchant who knew Saddam Hussain intimately due to the assistance he gave the Iraqi regime during the Iran-Iraq war. de-

spite this past record of help to the Iraqi people, his money and assets were seized on Saddam's orders. He received a death sentence.

Kuwaitis will never forget Al-

Mohamed Al-Fajji

Plate 95. An Iraqi truck attacked by Kuwaiti guerrillas during the early days of the invasion at the 4th Ring Road near Hawalli

Plate 96. A car used by Kuwaiti resistance fighters near the Kuwait International Hotel to assassinate Iraqi officials

Plate 97. Another Iraqi truck which fell victim to the resistance

Plate 98. An Iraqi truck attacked on the 5th Ring Road near Al-Jaberiya

96

Plate 99. An Iraqi tank hit by Kuwaiti guerrillas near the Sabah Al-Salem Bridge

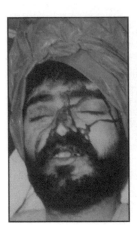

Plate 100. The martyr Saleh H. Saleh

Plate 101. A destroyed Iraqi troop carrier hit near the National Council building

Plate 102. The martyr Asrar Al-Qabandi's real driving licence...

Plate 103. ...The fake licence

Plate 104. Anti-personnel mines planted by the Iraqis near the Saudi border

Plate 105. Anti-aircraft gun used by the Iraqis during the allied air attack

Plate 106. A wire barrier erected by Iraqi troops near the Saudi border

مدينة الكويت
30
Kuwait City

Plate 107. Military check-points on a main road near Al-Massilah to show the readiness of Iraqi troops for war

Plate 108. Another military checkpoint on a flyover near Al-Qadisiyah

98

Plate 109. A girls secondary school in Rumaithiyah was an Iraqi special forces base

Plate 110. Barbed wire used to defend the beaches against an assault by allied marines

Plate 111. Trenches were laid everywhere along the beaches

Plate 112. Barbed wire and trenches at the beach in Salmiya

Al-Fajji with Saddam Hussain before the invasion - later Saddam ordered his execution

Fajji's record of service to his country. Not only did he support people with donations but his trucks were used to ferry goods from Iraq to Kuwait. He refused to yield to pressure from Sabaawi Ibrahim, chief of Iraqi intelligence, who asked him to collaborate forcing Al-Fajji to leave his home.

Al-Fajji formed one of the leading resistance units helped by Colonel Mahmoud Al-Dosari and Shaikh Athbi Fahd Al-Ahmed. Al-Fajji went to Iraq three times during the invasion where he gathered intelligence to help Kuwait. He was arrested with Al-Dosari at 10 a.m. on Wednesday 7 November 1990 and accused of attempting to overthrow the regime, financing the Kurdish rebels and assisting opposition in the south, as well as bribing officers and conspiring with two officials to assassinate Saddam. He was also charged with leading and financing resistance in Kuwait. Even just one of those charges was sufficient for a death sentence.

TRANSLATION
Republic of Iraq Presidency
Top Secret and Personal urgent
Number/2534
Date 21 October 1990
To head of the Intelligence Authority
To head of Special Security Authority
To head of General Security
To head of military intelliegence

Subject: Arrest
Based upon the important information which you sent on the escaped dangerous criminal Mohamed Mubarak Al-

Fajji, helped by the escaped dangerous criminal Mahmoud Mohamed Al-Dosari, the President ordered that efforts be concentrated to find and arrest them and inform us at once.

The letter from the head of the Intelligence Authority says that the above mentioned carry several forged IDs, are disguised and are causing huge damage because of what they are doing with the help of other criminals whom Al-Fajji met on his several visits to the country after 2 August 1990. He is the representative of Kuwait's Amir and Saad Abdullah Al-Salem and as the criminal enjoys a wide range of contacts in this country he is currently moving all over *the place and is financing traitors. the criminal is also the godfather of gangsters in the Kuwait governorate and has been leading them since the early days when the branch was returned to its roots. Start work on carrying out what is required.*

Copy to
Member of the country's
leadership
Ali Hassan Al-Majeed

Ahmed Hussein
Head of the Presidency

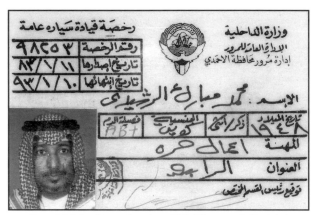

Forged driving licence found on Al-Fajji's arrest in Baghdad

▶ Secret newsletters

To combat the stream of false Iraqi propaganda, Kuwaiti journalists issued a number of newsletters to rebut the lies and distortions put about by the occupation forces. They urged nationals to resist with all their strength. Emanating from the resistance were Public Standfast, Al-Sabah and Kuwait Resistance group (KRG), while Voice of the Righteous was published in the mosques. One news bulletin reported an incident that occurred when an Iraqi officer was attempting to pay for an article at a shop but had insufficient money. A Kuwaiti stepped forward and paid the difference. The Iraqi officer was

صوت الحق

إفتتاحية

قال تعالى: « قل هو القادر على أن يبعث عليكم عذاباً من فوقكم أو من تحت أرجلكم أو يلبسكم شيعاً ويذيق بعضكم بأس بعض انظر كيف نصرف الآيات لعلهم يفقهون ». [سورة الأنعام]

وعن جابر رضي الله عنه قال: لما نزلت هذه الآية « قل هو القادر على أن يبعث عليكم عذاباً من فوقكم » فقال رسول الله صلى الله عليه وسلم: (أعوذ بوجهك) قال: « أو من تحت أرجلكم » قال: (أعوذ بوجهك). « أو يلبسكم شيعاً ويذيق بعضكم بأس بعض » فقال رسول الله صلى الله عليه وسلم: هذا أهون، أو هذا أيسر). أخرجه البخاري.

قوله « ومن فوقكم » كالحجارة التي أرسلت على قوم لوط، والماء المنهمر الذي أنزل على قوم نوح فأغرق قوم وغير ذلك. قوله « أعوذ بوجهك » النجي بوجهك. قوله « ومن تحت أرجلكم » كالخسف بقارون وإغراق آل فرعون. قوله « يلبسكم شيعاً » يجعلكم فرقاً مختالفين. « ويذيق بعضكم بأس بعض » يسلط بعضكم على بعض بالعذاب والقتل وغيره كما وقع في هذه الأيام. « والبأس »: القوة والشدة، وطلهم على الحرب والعذاب. قوله: (هذا أهون) أي فتنة الجن وتسليط بعضكم على بعض أهون من عذاب الله تعالى.

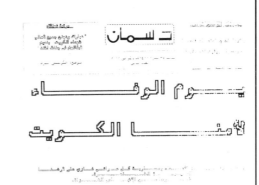

Two secret newsletters published by Kuwaitis during the occupation

moved and said:" By God, you are a generous man!" He subsequently surrendered his arms and uniform and deserted.

Many Kuwaitis were abused and tortured because of the newsletters. Newsletters began appearing from the day after the invasion. I saw the first as I left the mosque after Friday prayers on 3 August 1990. Many stopped at the beginning of the second week in September due to Iraqi surveillance and C.I.D. searches. Doctors, technical experts and engineers advised the bulletin writers on how householders should prepare for chemical attacks.

▶ Role of the mosques

The mosques were a focus for resistance. Residents of the neighbourhood would congregate at a mosque under cover of their religious observances but also would share news and offer mutual aid. The mosques were also safe havens in which to distribute money. The sense of community generated in the mosques brought Kuwaitis closer together and made them even more determined to resist Saddam Hussain's imperial ambitions.

▶ Animal rescue

A number of Kuwaitis made it their business to do everything possible to help the defenceless animals in Kuwait Zoo at Omariya. Two members of Al-Houti family did what they could to feed the beasts despite the humiliation and difficulties to which they were subjected by the Iraqis guarding the entrance.

Sulaiman Al-Houti

Ali Al-Houti

Sulaiman and Ali Al-Houti collected leftovers from the vegetable market and animal meat for the zoo collection and also tried to organise medical treatment.

▶ Shielding foreigners

On 21 August 1990 the Iraqis began rounding up western expatriates by force from their homes. Some fled to their embassies to avoid scrutiny by the plainclothes police. Many Kuwaiti families sheltered Europeans and Americans, or provided them with food, at grave risk to their lives. Top of the wanted list were Americans, Britons and French. A U.K. family remained hidden in a property in Ardiya throughout the occupation despite the fact that a search party actually entered the house. An American Muslim called Katherine was hidden by Mrs Roqay'yah Khalifa Al-Mutib at her home in Sabah Al-Salem district. They were both arrested on 10 January 1991 and Katherine was accused of spying. Happily both were freed.

▶ *Resistance from within*

Kuwaiti resistance fighters were ac-

Ruqqaya Al-Mit'ib and the American Muslim Katherine

tive in the first three months of the occupation. They often ambushed Iraqi buses coming from Basra and hit troop carriers and tanks in the city streets. The checkpoints were a favourite target after dark.

The slogan writers were also busy, attacking Saddam Hussain, denouncing the invasion and warning of the wrath to come for the Iraqis. The graffiti artists also affirmed the nation's loyalty to H.H. the Amir. The resistance concentrated on points where the Iraqis congregated using gas cylinders as bombs at the Kuwait International Hotel, the Orthology Roundabout, the Vegetable Market, the Kheitan area and Sulaibikhat Theatre.

The resistance had their eyes peeled for collaborators, especially those latterday Judases who informed the Iraqis where to arrest Kuwaiti officers and civil servants. Traitors were ambushed and assassinated, as happened with retired Brigadier Khudar Mubarek who was killed by guerrilla fighters from the resistance in the Rabiah area, after it had been confirmed beyond all reasonable doubt that he was implicated with the Baghdad regime. His burial took place at Sulaibikhat cemetery on 21 October 1990 under a protective cordon from Iraqi soldiers. In order to spread fear in the hearts of the craven Iraqi soldiers, snipers would open up at them when they entered residential areas. Towards the end Iraqis travelled always in groups, looking furtively to left and right with their weapons at the ready.

The Iraqi C.I.D. was quick to take

reprisals. They attacked houses near where their dead comrades were found, with hand grenades or Rocket Propelled Grenades (RPGs), as happened at Rawdah behind the Jamal Abdul Nasser Park.

The military governor of Kuwait Ali Hassan Al-Majeed was a resistance target. He was the target for more than one assassination attempt and telephone death threats. Because of the pressure on Al-Majeed, the Iraqi President appointed him Local Government Minister but he was rumoured to have remained in Kuwait throughout the occupation. He was seen with Saddam during his televised visit to Kuwait on 15 January 1991.

Lieutenant-Colonel Khalid S. Al-Fadil

One resistance fighter Captain Fahd Al-Shlaimi ambushed two armoured personnel carriers (APCs), carrying more than 30 men, at the top of a flyover in the Al-Qurain area. As the APCs passed below they were attacked with grenades by Al-Shlaimi and a comrade Talal Al-Azmi. The incident was recorded on video by a third man.

A young Kuwaiti girl evaded a checkpoint carrying weapons and RPG rounds. She reached two male colleagues who were waiting at a rendezvous near the Fahaheel Expressway where the road divides Mishrif and Bayan. The two men opened fire on Iraqi soldiers standing under the flyover opposite the Salwa area thanks to the weapons supplied by the girl courier. They all escaped after completing their mission.

Resistance fighters came from all age groups. A retired National Guard officer Lieutenant-Colonel Khalid Saud Al-Fadil, who fought with the Shaikh Athbi Fahd Al-Ahmed and Colonel Al-Dosari Group formed a unit of young men of not more than 17 who carried out several missions against the Iraqis at Kheitan and the Orthology Roundabout. They also worked as runners carrying information. Al-Fadil was a retired officer in the National Guard lately a civil servant in the military. He managed to escape arrest and was one of the first to spy on the Iraqis.

Mahmoud Mohamed Al-Dosari was head of security at Kuwait International Airport before the crisis. He headed one of the most active and important military units in resisting the Iraqi occupation. Saddam Hussein issued orders for his arrest.

A death sentence was passed on him and a colleague in Baghdad on 15 February 1991. Al-Dosari's fighters carried out their first operation in Iraq behind enemy lines by bombing the Sa'ad Palace in Basra and then made an attack on Al-Zobair. Several guerrilla attacks were mounted in Kuwait including attacks on restaurants where Iraqi soldiers dined.

The internal resistance sagged somewhat after November 1990 because of the mass arrests carried out by the Iraqis. Yet not all resistance was with weapons of war. A prayer leader at a local mosque, Jassim Mohalhal Al-Yaseen managed to gain the confidence of some of the Iraqi leaders in order to mediate and obtain the release of many detained Kuwaitis. He also had the courage to speak out against the rapes and theft carried out by the occupation forces.

The resistance also had a proud

Colonel Mahmoud Al-Dosari, head of the security department at Kuwait International Airport

record of war dead. Ahmed Mahmoud Qabazard, aged 32, was a captain serving in a VIP protection unit with the Ministry of Interior. He re-entered Kuwait disguised as a shepherd in the third week of the occupation and joined the Colonel Mahmoud Al-Dosari resistance group. His missions included blasting an Iraqi ammunition truck at Al-Jaberiya and other demolition jobs in Sulaibikhat. He was arrested on 7 September 1990 and executed in front of his home in Al-Jaberiya at 0900 on Sunday 16 September 1990, after which his home was burned to the ground. Before burying him at Sulaibikhat Cemetery his family noticed a huge wound in his thigh, his fingernails had been extracted and there were bullet holes in his head and neck.

A similar fate was meted out to Hamad Awad Rashid Al-Jowaisri, aged 20, a civil servant at the Minis-

The martyr Ahmed Qabazard with his daughter Shurouk

try of Public Works. He was detained on 12 September 1990 for attacking the Rumaithiya Police Station, carrying arms and killing Iraqi soldiers. Al-Jowaisri was executed by plainclothes police near his home in Rumaithiya on 20 September 1990. His older brother Rashid took his body to the local clinic. Hamad later died at the Mubarak Hospital after having his skull split open by an Iraqi who bludgeoned him with the butt of an AK-47.

Another resistance hero was Yousuf Khodair Yousuf Ali, aged 35, a captain in the 15th Brigade of the Kuwaiti Army. He killed a large number of Iraqi soldiers trapping them in houses in the Sabah Al-Salem and Al-Fintas neighbourhoods.

He was killed in action after he and comrades from the Massilah resistance group came under direct attack from three Iraqi tanks while sheltering in the Qurain area. He

The martyr Hamad Awad Al-Jowaisri

The martyr Yousef Khodair Ali with his two children

was hit by cannon fire in the head and back and died on 24 February 1991. He was buried in Sulaibikhat Cemetery the day after liberation.

▶ *Organising for victory*

Kuwaitis were sustained by a number of organisations which kept the spark of hope alive from within. Among them was the Kuwaiti Red Crescent which played a vital role, despite the detention of a number of its leading members. Active members included Abdul Karim Ja'ffar, Dr Ibrahim Behbehani, Dr Ibrahim Al-Shaheen, Dr Ali Al-Zuma'i, Dr Abdul Rahman Al-Mohailan, Dr Abdul Rahman Al-Sumait, Dr Adel Al-Falah and Mrs Dalal Al-Zabin.

Another more short lived organisation was formed from a joint group of civilian and military personalities. Among them were Shaikh Ali Salem Al-Ali, Shaikh Sabah Nasser Saud Al-Sabah, Shaikha Amthal Al-Ahmed Al-Jaber, General Khalid Boodai, Brigadier Yousuf Al-

Al-Massilah Group - the resistance centre at Al-Qurain where a number of Kuwaiti resistance fighters battled with Iraqi troops on 24 February 1991

Meshari, Brigadier Abdul Wahab Al-Muza'yyen (Retired), Colonel Fahd Al-Ameer, Colonel Mohammed Al-Haramy and Colonel Abdul-Aziz Barghash.

At the beginning of December 1990 a Supreme Committee was formed in Kuwait on a semi-official basis which included Shaikh Sabah Nasser Saud Al-Sabah, General Mohammed Al-Badr, General Khaled Boodai, Shaikh Ali Salem Al-Ali Al-Salem, Jassem Al-Aoun, Faisal Al-Marzouq, Abdul Wahab Al-Wazzan and Jawad Bu-Khamseen. This group was in secret contact with H.H. the Crown Prince in Taif and received important communications.

One aspect of internal military organisation was that resistance groups operated as independent cells, so that if information leaked only one group was broken up. Again it must be emphasised Ku-

waiti women were a vital link in the chain. Asrar Al-Qabandi penetrated the Kuwait-Saudi border more than three times to carry out information and bring back weapons. Asrar was the first woman guerrilla to make a link-up with Cable News Network (CNN) before her arrest. She paid the price with her life.

Among the resistance groups which played a dominant role in the fightback against the Iraqis was the group led by Colonel Fahd Al-Ameer, including Colonel Mohammed Al-Harami and Colonel Talal Al-Mosallam. Shaikh Athbi Fahd Al-Ahmed's group included Colonel Mahmoud Al-Dosari and Lieutenant-Colonel Khaled Soud Al-Fadel. Others included General Khaled Boodai's group, the team headed by General Mohammed Al-Badr, Khalid Al-Za'abi's group, and Massilah Group led by the martyr Sayyed Alawi.

Some acts of heroism have gone unrecorded, since they arose more out of the circumstances of war than any individual feats of arms. Shaikh Athbi, son of the martyr Fahd Al-Ahmed, was giving a presentation to resistance fighters on the mechanics of the Estrella missile when a short circuit took place and smoke erupted from the weapon. After evacuating his comrades, Shaikh Athbi carried the missile, threw it from the first floor window into the garden and managed to extinguish the source of the fire before it exploded.

I talked to a senior royal who took a leading role in co-ordinating the

Shaikh Sabah Naser Saud Al-Sabah - a key resistance leader

organisation of the country during the occupation. Shaikh Sabah Naser Al-Saud Al-Sabah (Abu Naser), was the assistant under-secretary of defence for military engineering installations and high on the Iraqi wanted list. He twice evaded the near certainty of capture. I asked him why he remained in the country, despite being a senior official and knowing he was the focus of a manhunt.

He replied: "I did not leave Kuwait for the same reason as you. Patriotic words are inadequate to answer your question. I stayed because my heart told me to do so. I was not alone. With me were my wife Shaikha Sabah Al-Salem Al-Sabah, who is sister to the Deputy Prime Minister and Foreign Minister Shaikh Salem Al-Sabah and Ali Salem Al-Ali, Ali Fahd Al-Salem who was taken prisoner just before liberation, Athbi Fahd Al-Ahmed, Dua'ij Salman Al-Du'aij, son of the former Justice Minister, Jaz'za Naser Al-Sabah and his two brothers Mohammed who was twice captured and Jaber and a whole host of others."

A rare photograph from 1963 when the then Iraqi President Abdul Karim Kassem threatened to annex Kuwait. The picture shows Shaikh Nasir Saoud Al-Sabah, father of the current Kuwaiti ambassador to Washington, surrounded by his bodyguards

They included Ali Abdulla Al-Khalifa, Hissah Sa'ad Al-Abdulla Al-Salem, daughter of H.H. The Crown Prince and Prime Minister, the two sisters Iqbal and Afdhal Dua'ij Al-Salman, May Abdulla Al-Jaber, Mishal Yousuf Saud Al-Sabah, the two brothers Khalid and Mohammed, Saleh Al-Mohammed, Khalid Fahd Al-Ahmed who was captured and then freed, Ahmed Al-Ali Al-Sabah and the two brothers Khalid and Abdulla Naser Al-Ali Al-Sabah, Mazen Al-Jarrah Al-Sabah and the brothers Dua'ij Naser and Salman Dawood Al-Salman Al-Sabah, Bibi Al-Ibrahim Al-Sabah, Sara Al-Ali Al-Sabah, Hamad Abdullah Al-Ahmed Al-Jaber and Fahd Salem Al-Ali the son of the head of the National Guard who is a prisoner-of-war.

Shaikh Sabah said that living with his family were Shaikha Amthal Al-Ahmed Al-Jaber Al-Sabah, the Amir's sister and Shaikha Awatif Sabah Al-Salem Al-Sabah, wife of the Kuwaiti ambassador to the U.S. Shaikh Saud Nasser Al-Sabah who left Kuwait a short time after the occupation to resume his diplomatic duties.

Abu Naser says:" My wife suffered a great deal by staying in Kuwait. All my efforts to persuade her to leave failed. I even thought about taking her away under sedation but to no avail. Sadly she even had a miscarriage because of an incident I was involved in with the Iraqis."

Shaikh Sabah recalls how he kept one step ahead of the Iraqis -- always on the run:" I moved house altogether 14 times. All Kuwaiti homes were open to me and I moved at will. I carried an incredible range of false papers, driving licences, civil I.D., passports and nationality cards. In each one I had a different job -- marketing manager of the General Trading Company, a merchant, an accountant at the Kuwait Danish Dairy Company and soon I had three different aliases -- Naser Saud Al-Mohammed, Mansour Ali Hussain Al-Khaja and Khalid Yousuf Al-Mohammed."

He says: "I will never forget what happened while I was staying in Mishrif at Ahmed Khaja's house. The area was surrounded for a search and the Iraqis entered the property and painstakingly went through all the rooms. I was interrogated and suspicions deepened as I was not the householder. At one point my wife had to speak to me briefly in English to remind me I had a resistance newsletter in my pocket. Unfortunately this was overheard by an Iraqi who told his superior:" Sir, there are foreigners in the house!"

I tried in vain to persuade the officer my wife was Kuwaiti and showed him her false I.D. -- Noora Mohammmed Al-Omani -- but he insisted I should go with them, together with my cousin Shaikh Mishal Yousuf Saud Al-Sabah. I was at first refused permission to speak to my wife but the officer relented and said, 'OK, leave that man who wants to be with his wife, leave him alone!' God's grace saved us but sadly the stress brought on my wife's miscarriage and for a week she was unable to move from her bed."

In a separate incident Abu Naser was stopped at a check point in a vehicle which was carrying 500,000 Iraqi dinars in the boot. The Iraqi officer began checking the car and asked about the money in the boot. Abu Naser answered coolly:" I am employed as a financial controller and here is a letter authorising me to carry large sums of money. Why don't you come to my company and check my credentials?" The officer refused the invitation and Abu Naser was saved from getting caught which might have resulted in execution if convicted.

Abu Naser headed a committee structure with three branches -- information, consultative and public services. Information brought together Advocate Abdulla Al-Ayoub, Sulaiman Al-Fahd, Salman Al-Dawood Al-Sabah, Toufik Al-Amir, Jawad Bu-Khamseen, Hussain Abdul Ridha and Abdullah Al-Muhailan. The consultative group studied local reaction to the Iraqi occupation authorities and ways of opposing them.

Its members included Dr Ibrahim Al-Khlaifi, Dr Anwar Al-Fuza'i, Abdul Aziz Al-Badr, Zuhair Al-Mazeedi, Mohammed Al-Ali and Fahd Al-Jalil. The services committee looked after electricity, water, gas, fuel and food supplies and there were also sub-committees on medical and transport affairs.

Abu Naser attributed the solidarity shown by Kuwaitis during the occupation crisis to their faith in God and trust in the family:" Kuwaitis were religious and stuck to their good practices and family loyalties. The government in exile's policies also helped. There were strategic food stocks available in Kuwait. Finally the government's wisdom in investing abroad proved its worth."

Abu Naser gave an account of how this shadow administration functioned during the occupation. He recalled:" We got information from three sources. The government in exile; our internal intelligence including Iraqi personnel and certain P.L.O. officers." The latter two gave us clues as to the whereabouts of Iraqi officials in Kuwait, army or special forces deployments and likely action by the Iraqis. Sometimes information had to be paid for -- amounts of between KD 50-2,000 depending on the importance of the tip off. We would either get this information to our sources outside the country by radio (easily traced by the Iraqis) or by satellite phones. About five of these were smuggled into Kuwait through Saudi Arabia in pick-up trucks hidden in water tanks.

A team of Ministry of Communications workers extracted from ministry stores under the noses of the invaders the very first satellite phone and gave it to our internal leadership. The first call was placed by Shaikh Ali Al-Salem Al-Sabah, oldest son of the head of the Kuwait National Guard. Shaikh Ali was out of Kuwait when the invasion occurred but returned on 4 August 1990 to work alongside his colleagues. Shaikh Ali was arrested and held at the Youth Prison at Sulaibiya

Shaikh Ali Salem Al-Ali Al-Sabah, the older son of H.E. the head of the National Guard in Kuwait, had played a major part in the resistance against the occupying forces

with a comrade in arms Ahmed Al-Wazzan. He had two civil I.D. cards with him in different names and managed to secure his release.

The satellite phones suffered a high rate of attrition. One broke down. A second was stolen in mysterious circumstances in the Rawdah area and two were seized by the Iraqis. The two remaining sets were used by the resistance to direct allied aircraft to targets during the air war. Colonel Naser Al-Farsi and Flight Commander Ama'ar Al-Ajmi took grave risks by keeping satellite equipment in their homes. Thanks to the expertise of Kuwaiti technicians the lines were kept open.

The allied command thanked specifically Shaikh Sabah Naser Saud Al-Sabah, General Khalid Boodai, Colonel Fahd Al-Ameer and Colonel Naser Al-Farsi for the intelligence

provided to the coalition forces. It saved allied lives and helped end the occupation more quickly.

▶ *Arab supporters*

The Arab expatriate community in Kuwait was divided during the occupation but some nationalities acted with honour towards their Kuwaiti hosts. A number of Egyptians fought with the resistance including Salamah Juma Hamida. Dr Abdul Halim Abdulla led anti Iraqi protests in the military hospital. Ibrahim Al-Shihabi salvaged the pupil attainment records from the Public Authority for Applied Education and Training which would almost certainly have been destroyed by the Iraqis.

Hamida, aged 35, was born in the Bani Suwaif Governorate of Egypt and was employed at the Kuwaiti Company for Pharmaceutical In-

Salamah J. Hamida - an Egyptian citizen who joined the resistance

dustries. His resistance work included acting as a courier for food and taking part in a raid on the main torture centre at Rabiah when a number of Iraqi guards were killed. He also blasted a truck loading soldiers under the Al-Ghazali flyover. I asked him why he did not flee as many other Egyptians had left. He replied:" How could I abandon a country when I had been living here and enjoying its hospitality and friendship. I couldn't possibly leave my Kuwaiti brothers to suffer at the hands of Saddam. Therefore, I swore before God to work with the Kuwaitis and either live among them or die."

Talib Abdul-Mohsin Al-Duhish, a Saudi citizen born in 1965, participated with his friends in resisting the Iraqis. He was wounded on 6 August 1990 by a bullet in his thigh.

Talib A. Al-Duhish - a Saudi citizen who joined the Kuwaiti resistance

On 2 January 1991 Al-Duhish, together with a group of Kuwaiti freedom fighters, was arrested and transferred to prison in Iraq from where he was later released after liberation.

Some of the Palestinians also worked with us. They helped safeguard the Salt and Chlorine factory as Abdul-Rahman Ghanayim and another Palestinian engineer kept the Doha Power Station going until it was sabotaged towards the end of the occupation. Another Palestinian family sheltered a female member of the Al-Sabah who was being hunted by the Iraqi C.I.D.. A Palestinian nurse at the Addan hospital risked her life with a colleague to offer treatment to wounded resistance fighters.

This, however, does not deny the fact that a number of Arab expatriates sold out to the enemy and turned their backs on the past kindnesses shown to them by Kuwaitis. The collaborators are known but we must never forget those expatriates who stood by us.

DELIVERANCE AND SADDAM'S FINAL SOLUTION

The 40 days from the beginning of the air war at first light on 17 January 1991 until liberation on 26 February 1991 were indeed dark days for all Kuwaitis. The country became a prison. Citizens literally battened down their hatches and lived through most of that time in constant anxiety. They shut themselves in their rooms or huddled together in underground shelters.

The air strikes were ceaseless. Allied aircraft raided the Iraqi forces in Kuwait and hit military targets at will but in the meantime Iraq's campaign of terrorism against the civilian population of Kuwait reached its peak. Nationals were pulled from the streets. Every knock on the door was enough to fill our hearts with fear. The Iraqis knew they could not keep Kuwait so they decided on a "final solution" to destroy the whole country.

Iraqi trench on Salmiya beach

114

▶ *Saddam's soldiers make ready*

Saddam Hussain's army dug in for war. His sappers built five defensive lines constructed from trenches, landmines, barricades and moats filled with oil, stretching the extent of the southern and western borders with Iraq and Saudi Arabia. The Iraqi director of military inspection General Saadi Saleh To'ma who supervised this "Iraqi Maginot Line" was rewarded by his leader with the Defence Ministry portfolio in the Iraqi cabinet.

The Iraqis also mined the oil fields, oil installations, refineries and power and desalination plants. Trenches, barricades and barbed wire were laced along the Kuwait shoreline, since Saddam Hussain believed the allies would strike with amphibious

An underground bunker for the Iraqi commander close to Al-Mitla'a

landings. The occupation forces also installed anti-aircraft guns on the principal flyovers and even sited them on the tops of buildings in residential areas. From 8 January 1991 the flyovers were sealed with concrete blockades and surveillance posts were positioned there. Pill boxes were erected at the entrances to the main residential areas. Empty or half finished houses were commandeered and sand-bagged. Large picture windows were sealed with concrete breeze blocks. From 17 January 1991 street lights in both the major and minor roads were extinguished. In the meantime a complex network of field telephones was laid out for use in the event of communications being cut. Finally a total of some 5 million mines were planted on land and at sea. Saddam Hussain made two morale raising visits to Kuwait -- the first to the northern borders in early January 1991 and the last to his troops at Salmiya on 15 January 1991.

▶ *Kuwaitis prepare for war*

Many citizens had readied themselves for war as early as September 1990 when rumours spread about a possible Iraqi gas attack similar to the massacre of the Kurds at Halabjah in 1988. Serious preparations began on Friday 11 January 1991 when "Kuwait Message", a television programme broadcast from some of the other Gulf states, included items about do-it-yourself preparations for war.

The next day Kuwaitis built shelters in their houses or flats with wa-

Plate 113. Underground reservoir used for ammunition storage

Plate 114. Another ammunition storage point

Plate 115. Trenches and observation points on the beaches at Salmiya

Plate 116. Underground trench at Salmiya - Iraqi troops smashed up window frames and inserted breeze blocks as a defence

Plate 117. The residential complex at Al Fintas - looted and wrecked

Plate 118. A private home at Al Fintas - changed into a museum

Plate 119. The modified Scud missile called Al-Abbas found at the Al-Wafra area

Plate 120. Many Iraqi soldiers surrendered in the first days of the liberation

Plate 121. A distant view of oil fire horrors.

Plate 122. On the route between Matla'a and Abdali: Saddam's dreams are shattered.

Plate 123. A Kuwaiti military vehicle on the road to Kuwait on 26/2/91 going through a route dug out of minefields, by the allies, on the Kuwait/Saudi border.

Plate 124. An Iraqi tank near the Centre for Disabled in the Sulaibikhat area.

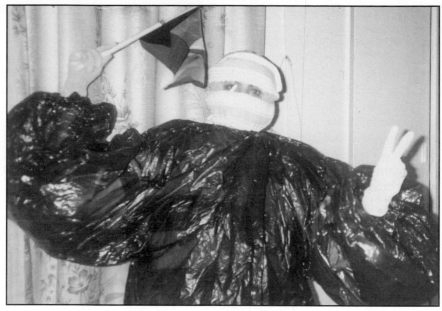

A young Kuwaiti wearing a plastic shield to protect himself from an expected Iraqi chemical attack

ter, tinned food, radios, torches, medicines and first aid kits. Some citizens obtained Atropine serum for injecting themselves as an antidote to nerve gas. A few underground shelters were equipped as mini-hospitals.

▶ The air war starts

The U.N. Security Council issued Resolution No 678 on 29 November 1990, allowing Iraq a grace period to withdraw from Kuwait until midnight on Tuesday 15 January 1991 Eastern Standard Time (0700 on Wednesday 16 January 1991 in Kuwait). After that all necessary means would be taken by the allies to expel the Iraqis from Kuwait.

As 16 January dawned the Iraqis appeared unrepentant. Nineteen

An American pilot who flew with the coalition forces

hours after the deadline expired the liberation war began. I was awakened by the telephone at 0300 on Thursday 17 January 1991. My sister told me the allies had started bombing Baghdad. I didn't believe it but the Sawt Al-Arab radio station in Cairo confirmed its veracity. Ascending to the roof of my house at 0315 I saw Triple A (anti-aircraft fire) illuminating the sky in the Mishrif and Bayan areas.

I passed the news to the rest of the family. We gathered in the protected room on the ground floor and our hearts were filled alternately with hope and fear. We prayed earnestly that God would deliver us from the horrors of war. For 24 hours we remained shuttered up while all around us air raids erupted with the sounds of cannon and automatic weapons firing in response. No sooner had one of us dropped off to sleep than a new air raid would start.

One morning a group of resistance fighters at Rumaithiya surrounded the Umm Salama Intermediate Girls School where the Iraqi militia had based themselves and opened fire. A large number of them surrendered and began handing over their weapons. A counter-attack then took place, involving a detachment of special forces, the Iraqi C.I.D. and police. The guerrillas were in turn surrounded and caught. Four were summarily executed. Their bodies were dumped in the street near the O'mama Bint Bishr Secondary School. The premature attack may have been motivated by irresponsible reports from certain news agencies that the air war would only last a matter of days.

▶ *Escalation of air attacks*

The air raids were resisted by both mobile and stationary anti-aircraft batteries. In time nationals got used to the noise and many started to observe the course of the battle from their rooftops. Most coalition aircraft flew at such high altitudes that the enemy air defences were useless. The Iraqi air force was nowhere to be seen.

The first clear sighting of an allied sortie over Kuwait City was at 1215 on Thursday 17 January 1991. Seven aircraft flew in at high altitude from the west travelling eastwards along the coast. Rumours were rife. The coalition forces were said to be in control of two bridgeheads at Nuwaiseeb; Failaka island had been liberated; a Kuwaiti Air Force plane had been shot down at the Burgan oil field but the pilot was safe.

The only day without air attacks was Friday 8 February 1991 but few nationals felt any relief. The heaviest raids on Kuwait were made by the giant American B-52 bombers which hit the city from 2000 hours on 31 January 1991 until 1600 the next day.

The pattern of regular air raids continued into February. On 2 February 1991 Kuwaitis heard for the first time the anti-aircraft batteries in the Salmiya beach area following strikes by Tornado aircraft on Failaka island.

As a result of these repeated attacks many of the targets occupied by the Iraqis were destroyed in-

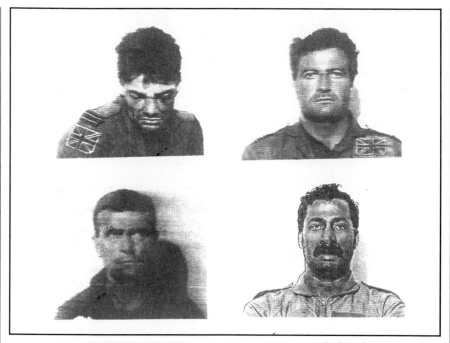

A Kuwaiti Air Force pilot Lieutenant-Colonel Mohamed Mubarak paraded with other captured allied pilots on Iraqi TV

A stolen Armoured Personnel Carrier (APC) buried near the coast at Bneid Al-Qar

Damage at the Kuwait Danish Dairy Company

Air attacks on Kuwait were directed at Iraqi troop concentrations.

A cluster bomb used on the Iraqis by coalition forces and found in the Al-Mila'a area

cluding the notorious building used as a torture centre by the C.I.D. but actually belonging to the General Corporation for Agriculture and Fisheries. Others hit included the Communications buildings at Safat and Sabahiya, Al-Nassr Club in Jleeb Al-Shuyoukh, an ammunition dump in the Subhan Industrial Area and the doctors residence at the Addan Hospital. Due to precision bombing very little collateral damage occurred to civilians living near the targets.

Failaka island, already abandoned by the Iraqis, was subjected to a violent bombardment by coalition warships for three hours from 2000 on Wednesday 20 February 1991.

I met Major Khalid Al-Za'abi from the Kuwaiti Air Force who played a distinguished role in bombing col-umns of Iraqi forces advancing on Kuwait on 2 August 1990 and asked him about the start of the air war. He said:" My colleagues and I were unaware of when zero hour would be. Our instructions were to prepare aircraft and arm them in the after-noon of Wednesday 16 January 1991, a few hours before the eventual at-tack. The reason was obvious enough -- to maintain secrecy and take advantage of surprise. I was detailed various targets to hit in Kuwait including a Scud missile launcher installed in a park south of Sabahiya. Several sorties were aimed at the same target to ensure its full destruction. I often had to wait more than 45 minutes to take off as sorties were being launched at the rate of one mission a minute."

The damage at the Shuwaikh power and desalination plant

▶ *Propaganda battle resumes*

The Iraqis hit back with a resumption of the propaganda war. The Mother of Battles Radio Station began transmitting false reports and communiques on the course of the fighting. As the air waves praised Saddam Hussain, his forces were engaged in an orgy of rape and atrocities against civilians. As the Iraqi air force fled to Iran, or remained grounded in hardened shelters in Iraq, communiques boasted each day of dozens of allied aircraft shot down.

When the Iraqis attacked the Saudi border town of Khafji on 30 January 1991, the Iraqis claimed it was the beginning of a campaign to free Najd and Hejaz (names used before the unification of the kingdom of Saudi Arabia by Ibn Saud). By then Saudi and Qatari forces who counter-attacked strongly were driving the Iraqis out of Khafji and mopping up stragglers.

The Iraqis in Kuwait actually believed these lies and cheered in the streets at the announcements of a "great victory." The Iraqis used school loudspeaker systems to broadcast their news and turned them up especially loud at Friday prayer times.

▶ *Services are cut*

Power was cut off in Kuwait for the first time since the start of the air war on 15 February 1991 only to be restored 24 hours later. Interruptions continued intermittently until 0400 on Sunday 24 February 1991 when they became permanent as sabotage started at the power stations and sub-stations. I awoke that morning to terrible explosions emanating from the oil transformers at the junction of the Fifth Ring Road with Fahaheel Motorway. It was one of scores of sub-stations blasted by the retreating rabble.

Internal telephone communications were cut in some suburbs, Al-Firdous, Al-Andalus, Al-Riqq'ee and Al-Ardiya on the evening of Saturday 19 January 1991. They were totally disrupted with effect from the night of Thursday 7 February 1991, possibly to improve the Iraqi forces chances of moving around without detection.

Water was also cut off. The flow reduced drastically from 6 February 1991 onwards and broke down completely on 10 February 1991. Drinking water tankers charged inflated prices and the tanker owners insisted on having their fuel tanks filled with petrol before they would sell water.

▶ *Pollution on land and sea*

At 1800 on 24 January 1991 the sky over Kuwait turned red as the Iraqis detonated the northern pier of the Mina Al-Ahmadi oil terminal in Abu Halifa. A huge quantity of oil leaked into the sea. The 11 million barrels spillage was one of the largest oil pollution disasters in the history of the sea and will leave a legacy of habitat destruction that will last generations. The Iraqis were confident that the allied attack would

The pipeline used by the Iraqis to transport crude oil to the Gulf

Damage at an oil gathering centre at Mina Al-Ahmadi North

Exploding oil wells viewed from the 7th Ring Road in Kuwait

Ground fires near one of the sabotaged wells

A dramatic view of the oil field catastrophe in Kuwait

The impact of air pollution from blazing oil wells at the front of a Kuwaiti home

126

come from the sea -- a gross miscalculation of General Schwarzkopf's strategy.

This was accompanied by the blasting of more than 730 oil wells as part of Saddam Hussain's scorched earth policy. Initial estimates of lost revenue were about $1.44 million a day. After that the $2 billion costs of the fire fighting operation, completed in November 1991, have to be taken into account, together with the long-term threat to health from air pollution. I first saw the tell tale thick black smoke for the Maqwa, Burgan and Ahmadi oil fields on Sunday 2 February 1991 and on Monday 11 February 1991 thick acrid smoke blacked out Kuwait City. Day had become night. On 24 February 1991 darkness again descended as the Iraqis continued to detonate wells in mass panic at the wrath to come.

Abdul Latif Al-Kharaza

▶ First hint of withdrawal

The first hint of an Iraqi withdrawal came on Friday 15 February when Baghdad Radio expressed a qualified readiness to deal with Security Council Resolution 660. The Iraqi troops were elated even asking Kuwaiti citizens to join them in spontaneous demonstrations. Disillusion soon set in. The soldiers realised they would not be going home before facing a day of reckoning with the allies. Food supplies were getting low and prices were increasing.

Life had begun to return to normal after the first 10 days of the air war. Most Kuwaitis were forced to travel around on foot as the Iraqis

had announced the confiscation of all vehicles with Kuwaiti plates. Some citizens took to their bicycles. Others who had cars with Iraqi registrations helped distribute food. Cooking gas was in short supply and wood had to be used instead. Some co-operatives closed or only opened one day a week. Food queues began to lengthen. Enormous efforts were made by Abdul Latif Al-Kharaza, chairman of the Association of Co-operative Societies, and his fellow directors to keep the food chain intact. Al-Kharaza's work was often hampered by Iraqi harasssment.

▶ Theft and arrests on a grand scale

The Iraqis embarked on a final orgy of theft. Not content with merely taking Kuwaiti registered cars off the streets they began looking in garages and parking bays. Any Kuwaiti who stood in their way was arrested on the spot. Petrol was siphoned from tanks as the allies had by then reduced fuel supplies to virtually zero with their air attacks.

As soon as the Kuwait liberation campaign started, the Iraqis began randomly picking up nationals in the streets. This reached a peak on the week-end of 21-22 February 1991. One friend was even arrested for not wearing a seat-belt. After Friday prayers on 22 February thousands were arrested while leaving the mosques.

President Bush's final deadline of Saturday 23 February for Iraq to retreat from Kuwait (following the failed Soviet initiative) passed quietly in Kuwait. It was 0400 on Sunday 24 February 1991 when Kuwaitis first heard news of the land attack although it was later learned that the allies had penetrated Iraq for General Norman Schwarzkopf's left-hook encircling movement as early as Friday 22 February 1991.

President Bush - liberator

Dr Ahmed Bakir - arrested

▶ *Last days of horror*

Saddam Hussain, by now hiding in his presidential bunker, ordered a rapid escalation in the campaign of attrition against Kuwaitis. All nationals were to be snatched from the streets. Kuwaiti men were to be killed. Chemicals weapons were to be used. I saw a drawing in the information centre at Jaberiya showing the sites to be destroyed with chemical weapons. A newspaper published on 26 February 1991 revealed the text of a document showing that chemical weapons were to be used to kill defenceless Kuwaitis. A friend Walid Bishara saw two bombs, one at Farwaniya and the other at Salmiya, with "Danger -- Chemical" written on them.

Dr Ahmed Bakir, the former National Assemblyman, was one of the Kuwaitis arrested in the final purge. He subsequently treated sick Kuwaitis in the Abu Skhair Detention Centre in Iraq. He was detained on

Friday 22 February 1991 and was freed two weeks later. He recalls: "On my way to Friday prayers an Iraqi stopped my car and hauled me off for questioning at Surra Police Station. I was kept at the Youth Prison until midday on Monday 25 February 1991 when I was moved with 1,200 other Kuwaitis to the Abu Skhair P.O.W. camp at Basra. We were held in four hangars, each being of not more than 35X5 metres.

"Due to the overcrowding there was no way anyone could sleep. The floors were of cement with no shelter from the cold. We had to cling together for warmth. Water was in short supply. It was supplied in a polluted form full of worms once a day. Our people were falling sick with diarrhoea and internal bleeding at the rate of five to 10 a day -- the diagnosis of dysentery. I was allowed to travel with the sick to the Basra Military Hospital under escort and bring back medicine. The only meals were a small quantity of rice mixed with dirt and stale bread."

Among the VIPs in the detention camp were another former M.P. Abdullah Al-Roomi; Saud Al-Talab, deputy personnel commissioner; Khalid Al-Saleh former under-secretary of housing; Faisal Al-Marzouq, editor-in-chief of the daily Al-Anba; Mahmoud Mohammed Al-Ghanim, a leading businessman; Dr Ghanim Al-Najjar from Kuwait University and Dr Badr Al-Shibani, member of the Public Authority for Applied Education and Training.

During the last four days of the occupation the Iraqis set fire to or set off explosions at many institu-

Damage at the Kuwait Sheraton

Damage at the SAS Hotel

*Damage at the
Meridien Hotel*

*Damage at the
Al-Salam Hotel*

tions and public buildings. We would wake to hear new blasts at hotels, power stations, leisure centres and electricity sub-stations. From 2100 on Monday 25 February 1991 Iraqi Triple-A and cannon fire escalated in a horrifying way in response to allied air and sea bombardment. We were close to death but hours later deliverance was at hand.

▶ Withdrawal from Kuwait

The craven withdrawal of the Iraqi army from Kuwait was an unforgettable event. At 2200 on Monday 25 February 1991 I saw an unusual gathering of civilian vehicles at the check point near my home overlooking the Fahaheel Motorway. Iraqi C.I.D. with automatic weapons got out of these stolen vehicles and then left at speed. From 2300 on the same evening until 0200 the next morning (26 February 1991) there was intense northwards traffic movements on the Fahaheel Expressway. Hundreds of Iraqi vehicles, tanks, APCs, and trucks were moving at high speed. Lorries full of soldiers began leaving the schools often pursued by desperate militia men on foot trying to get aboard. One fell off but his screams were ignored in the panic of flight. In Salmiya thousands of cowardly Iraqis rushed the departing convoys begging for a safe passage from Kuwait and abandoned their weapons and equipment.

The actual withdrawal had started at 1900 on Monday 25 February 1991 but was not officially acknowledged until 0230 the next day in a broadcast monitored by Damascus Radio.

I could hardly credit it. Were these the brave soldiers with whom Saddam Hussain planned to challenge the entire international community? From the evidence of their helter-skelter head over heels flight the Iraqis were indeed cowards. The bully boys had got their come uppance and many met their deaths in the allied air force's killing ground between Al-Mitla and Al-Abdali. Soldiers, equipment and weapons were destroyed there but among the charred remains were also found the evidence of wholesale theft and robbery by Saddam's criminal rabble.

▶ Lessons from the crisis

Kuwaitis must thank God for their deliverance and pray for the souls of the martyrs. Our first thoughts are for the return of missing prisoners of war so their families may be brought relief. Undoubtedly many lessons will be learned from the occupation and liberation.

It proved beyond doubt the deep patriotism of all Kuwaitis and their loyalty to the legitimate leadership of H.H. The Amir Shaikh Jaber Al-Ahmed Al-Sabah. Our citizens refused to collaborate with the Iraqis and this solidarity is a true foundation for the future development of Kuwait.

The occupation proved the need for practical education and training in Kuwait. During the seven months from August 1990 to February 1991 Kuwaitis learned new skills and were forced to undertake jobs that former-

Tank ammunition found hidden near the beach at Bida'a

ly they had considered beneath them.

This enterprise should be exploited. Secondary and higher education curriculums require new strategies to provide the necessary technical abilities for the next generation in power and water, public works, healthcare and many others.

The reconstruction period will also provide an opportunity to reappraise Kuwait's administration as well as its bilateral relationships with foreign states. These must be prioritised according to mutual interests for the long-term benefit of Kuwait.

The occupation also exposed weaknesses in Kuwait's security arrangements due to the government's past concern to be a good neighbour and give other countries "the benefit of the doubt." Any reappraisal here must be done objectively and with regard to political realities. For the occupation has shown that Kuwait can no longer be ruled by the heart where its vital interests are concerned. ∎

INDEX

134